THE FOURTEENTH MAN AT DINNER

MARILYN SMITH PORTER

Copyright © (2025) Marilyn S. Porter
All rights reserved. No portion of this book may be reproduced or transmitted by any means- electronic, mechanical, photocopy, recording, or otherwise without the prior written permission of the copyright owner.

Marilyn S. Porter
Marilynsporter1217@gmail.com
Paperback ISBN: 979-8-9929138-0-4
Editor: Abigail L. Gonzalez
Cover Designed by: Victoria Lauren Bryan

TABLE OF CONTENTS

THE FOURTEENTH MAN AT DINNER	4
NO BODY, NO HARM, NO FOUL	57
THE WORD OF THE WINDOW WASHER WITNESS	82
WHAT THE BLIND MAN SAW	106

THE FOURTEENTH MAN AT DINNER

Introducing: Detective Nick Tracy

SOUTHAMPTON, LONG ISLAND, N.Y., DECEMBER 1978

8:07 A.M

The workmen came somewhat "unhinged" at the sight of what looked like a BODY. Nothing more than skeletal remains wedged in the hidden closet's corner. The men were there for the demolition of the old mansion; removing dead bodies was not part of their job description. They gathered around, staring at the scene as Jim Reeves, the oldest among them, took credit for the discovery.

"There it was. I thought it was just one of those fake Halloween props," Reeves stated.

But real or not, what did it matter? Remove the bones and continue working. Everyone waited for instructions while the foreman used the kitchen phone to call the local police department.

8:21 A.M

Homicide Detective Nick Tracy stepped out of the library, where the demolition crew had found the body. Tracy, an honest-to-goodness-real-life detective looked more like a big movie star playing a detective, had perfected the long stride as he walked through the hall of the empty mansion, a neo-gothic structure that reminded Detective Tracy of the settings in his favorite classic black-and-white movies, where the murder was always committed on a dark and dreary night, with lightning illuminating rooms and grisly faces. The mansion didn't look so menacing in the light of day, but Tracy could imagine that a cold rainy night might bring out the worst in the old girl.

Tracy turned to the man on his right. Officer Jones, who was from the local precinct, accompanied him to the scene. Tracy was unfamiliar with Jones, since he was on loan for this case. "Okay, Patrolman. I'm done in the library. Your guys can remove the corpse. Maybe the coroner can give us some answers." Tracy remarked.

As Officer Jones left to retrieve the medical examiner's team, Tracy glanced down at his notes. Judging by the clothing, he assumed the stiff was male. He searched the pockets of the man's red-stained coat and pants; there was no wallet or form of identification, only a set of keys in the right-hand pants pocket. Tracy had suspicions about who the dead man was. If he were right, it would answer the $64,000 question on everyone's mind: Where was John H. Roth, the wealthy businessman who had never shown up at a party in this very house and then disappeared from the face of the earth one year ago, December 17, 1977?

Perhaps Mr. Roth hadn't missed the party after all. Over the past twelve months, extensive searches at home and abroad and significant media coverage had not uncovered clues about Mr. Roth's whereabouts. Speculators alleged that he was concealing himself to avoid tax issues and the consequences of poor business decisions. Others suggested a woman was involved. His wife disputed these rumors but offered no alternative explanation. This discovery would be big news if these skeletal remains were, in fact, John Roth.

But of course, it would also raise additional questions like: was there foul play? It was clear the corpse hadn't wedged himself into that library closet. He must have had help.

    The New York City detective turned and set out across the wide hallway, back into the empty library. He took one last look around at the massive room with the hidden closet that had held its secret for over a year and evaluated his chances of solving this case. Every detective on every homicide in every city had to ask themselves a few basic questions at the start of any investigation, but none of those questions would be answered on this one. After a year, physical evidence was going to be minimal: no murder weapon, no stomach contents, no fingerprints, no witnesses. Without any help from the victim, this crime would take reasoning, imagination, and much help from the living. If the bones turned out to be John Roth, Tracy knew precisely where to begin his investigation, just as they did in the early black-and-white movies before the 1970s, when technology had turned detective work into mechanics.

    Yes. He would begin... at the beginning.

* * *

"Alright, Mr. DeMille. I'm ready for my close-up."
-Sunset Blvd. (1950)

    It's been three days since the discovery of John Roth's body. At the Southampton precinct, Detective Nick Tracy started reviewing the list of partygoers to refresh his memory about what happened that night a year ago. The file included a list of names and a New York social registry page with the words "Who's Who." But which one among them was a killer? One of them was. Tracy made a note after each name.

THE PARTY GUEST LIST:

Beatrice (Bitsy) Roth	The victim's third wife
James Howell III	The owner of the mansion, host
Constance Howell	Wife of James, hostess
Zuzu Gabbard	Famous fashion designer
Lawrence Winthorpe	J. Roth's friend and financial advisor
Drake Carrington	Middle aged land baron
Christina Carrington	Wife of Drake, socialite
Theodore Carlisle	Friend, old money
Douglas Winston	Insanely rich international playboy
Richard Crawley	Wealthy businessman
Dora Crawley	Wife of R. Crawley, British-born socialite
Devin Thielberg	Hollywood mogul, movie producer

THE HOUSEHOLD EMPLOYEES:

Reginald	The Butler/Houseman
Melanie R.	The Cook
Penelope S.	The Server

Tracy closed his notebook with a snap and checked over the coroner's report. There was no longer any doubt. The dental records confirmed that what was left of the corpse belonged to Mr. John Roth. The dark red stain down the front of the clothing was analyzed. Mr. Roth had been dead, residing in that secret closet for a year. The mansion had been vacated the day after "the party," according to the Howells; no one had been through the doors until the remodel had started a few days ago. Twelve months. Very convenient.

There was no chance of anyone getting a whiff of decaying flesh or stumbling upon the body. There was no chance of anyone formulating ideas about Mr. Roth's disappearance. Detective Tracy clicked his tongue in annoyance and opened his notebook again:

1. No help from forensics. Corpse a year old.
2. A demolition crew almost destroyed the scene of the crime.
3. Hazy witnesses memories of what happened the night of the party.
4. No trace of a murder weapon and no hope of finding one.
5. Several "suspects" have now had one year to shore up details.

Tracy glanced at the list of partygoers. Unorthodox murders called for unorthodox methods. He would gather everyone who attended the party that night, including the staff, and take them to the old mansion as the backdrop. He would recreate the scene. It may jog memories. James Howell III, the mansion's owner, cooperated with the investigation. He granted Tracy complete freedom; the mansion was at his disposal. This was not a case of death by natural causes. Tracy was convinced that someone at the party that night had killed the missing millionaire. Someone on this list was a killer.

The detective grabbed his coat, turned out the light, and shut the office door behind him. It was late; most in the precinct had gone home for the night, home to wives and families. Tracy had neither; he was a confirmed bachelor, now forty-seven years old and set in his ways. But when he wanted to, he could attract females. Oh, yes. He had the tools. A frame that was a notch or two above six feet on the tape measure, dark wavy hair graying at the temples, a well-proportioned build, and a rugged face with a jaw that could cut paper.

Some of the guys at the Manhattan station had dubbed him the "Rock Hudson of the east side precincts." Others had remarked that he resembled his old cartoon "namesake." The one in the yellow trench coat, the deeply creased fedora, and the two-way radio watch on his arm. Maybe someday he would settle down. But for now, this was 1978, rapidly approaching the dawn of '79, and Tracy was firmly married to a job that needed his undivided attention.

Til death do us part.

* * *

"So help me God."
-Scarlett O'Hara in Gone with the Wind

They were all there, wearing their social faces and forced smiles, as they sat on folding chairs in a semi-circle inside the great hall, now stripped of its finery; cold and empty, so unlike the former glory days when the gothic structure had been alive with the sounds of music and laughter. The owners of the mansion, the Howells, were well known for throwing lavish soirees and over-the-top galas that graced the Society Page of the New York Times. Even though none of the people in the empty hall brought up the subject, they all remembered THAT night a year ago. December 1977...

It had been cold, bone-chilling cold, and threatening snow. Within the mansion, the fires roared inside the honey-hued fireplaces, and their thickly carved mantles were adorned for the upcoming Christmas season. Ten-foot spruce trees lined the great hall with bright ornaments and colored lights. Soft music played in the background. There were no dramatic episodes like that one year, Doreen Crawley, bless her heart, threw an expensive glass of white wine in Zuzu Gabbard's face during the lingering dessert course of truffles.

Or the year that the Carringtons, Drake and Christina, had duked it out verbally after too many rum-and-cokes, their drink of choice. This party had been uneventful, and they all remembered it that way, right to the last person, until the following morning when it was discovered that John Roth was missing. Today, they sat quietly as everyone looked at each other with curiosity. Over the past twelve months, they spent a lot of time talking among themselves, reflecting on their memories, speculating, and awaiting answers that never arrived. The topic of the missing John Roth was all but forgotten.

Everyone turned in unison as Detective Nick Tracy, the one handling the case, entered the room. He stood before them, thanking them for their attendance and cooperation with his investigation. A sea of heads nodded silently as he glanced around at the assembled elite of society; Tracy felt a sensation. Anyone remotely acquainted with Tracy knew he was obsessed with the detective and mystery genres of the early 1930s and 1940s. He watched classic old movies during solitary dinners at home and on his days off. A few years ago, he realized that someone in each of his cases would remind him of one of those old thrillers.

Turning to Reginald Carter, the Howells' butler, Tracy said, "Please follow me." The assembled individuals lingered behind, shivering and grumbling about the cold in the empty, dimly lit hall as they awaited their turn for interrogation. Underneath it all, they pondered: What happened in this house? Is John Roth's murderer present in this room?

***
"The butler did it"
(words attributed to every film noir but never uttered)

The butler sat perfectly still on a wooden crate left behind by the demolition crew. Reginald Carter was the classic ramrod-straight, gray-haired manservant who graced every detective film. He was impeccably dressed, with not a hair out of place or a random stain on his starched red tie.

"Okay, let's review this again, Mr. Carter. Are you sure Mr. Roth left this house BEFORE the party guests arrived? You say that you didn't show him out yourself."

Reginald Carter nodded firmly. There was no doubt in his mind until he suddenly jumped and began to tap his feet in place. Tracy chose to ignore the tapping and continued. .....

"And everyone in the great hall is the same people who were here the night of the party on December 17, 1977? And none of them were in this house when Mr. Roth was here?"

Reginald nodded more forcibly this time. When he spoke, he shifted to a ball-change step. "I am certain, Detective. I know because I let everyone in through the front door that night long after Mr. Roth left. And I can vouch for the staff. No question."

"Okay, Reginald, what can you tell me about the rooms that night? I understand some of the furnishings had been removed and put in storage."

"The upstairs was empty. Mr. and Mrs. Howell had already removed everything from the private quarters. Downstairs, a few of the rooms were still furnished; the public areas."

"Where were the Howells sleeping?" Tracy asked.

"They moved into their apartment in town. This house was entirely emptied the day after the party.

Demolition was scheduled for spring, but a few problems arose.

"I get the picture, Reginald. No one went upstairs that night that you know of?"

"No, sir. I would have seen them if they did."

"What about the library? Did anyone go in or come out before or after dinner?"

"Yes. Mr. Winston went in before dinner. I didn't see Mrs. Roth go in, but I saw her come out once. Mr. Carlisle, Mr. Crawley, and Mr. Howell went in sometime during the party to settle a bet. There were some reference books on the shelf that they needed to consult."

"And now about the deceased, Mr. Roth, you say you let him in about half an hour before the party."

"Yes, sir. He dropped a note for Mr. Howell and placed it in the library on the desk. I saw it there myself."

Detective Tracy conjured up a picture he had seen once of John Roth. A man who was a bit on the short and stocky side with a permanent day-old growth of beard and a crop of hair in need of a cut. A harsh and uneven bloke. Sort of a John Garfield character. (People remembered Garfield in movies he had never been in. Or in love affairs that he had never known.) The Detective continued with his questioning. "I noticed in the original report from last year you said Mr. Roth arrived in a taxi. You may remember Mr. Roth's car was found in the country club parking lot six blocks the next day. Did Mr. Roth explain why he had chosen to hire a cab and not bring his car such a short distance?"

"Yes, sir. When he saw me looking at the waiting taxi, he mentioned he didn't like to drive while taking his migraine medication. It rendered him unable to operate machinery, including his car.

"And when did Mr. Roth leave the premises?"

"When I left to get the alcoholic beverages and returned, he was already gone."

"How do you know he left?"

"Penelope, sir. She showed him out the front door while I was in the wine cellar."

"And you believe this, Miss Penelope? Has she ever tried to cover her tracks?"

The butler shook his head. He stopped dancing. "No, sir. A year ago, when the police questioned her about being the last person to see Mr. Roth alive, Miss Penelope told the same story I just told you. She has never wavered. I believe her."

"Reginald, that's all for now. I may have some questions later."

The butler started for the door that led back to the grand hall. He turned…"I was sorry to hear that Mr. Roth was found in the library closet, sir. I liked him very much. And I know you have to suspect everyone; that's your job. However, this is NOT a case where the butler did it. I can assure you of that."

"Okay, Reginald, then who, in your opinion, DID do it? You told me you've been working in this house for twenty-three years. Between you and me and officially off the record, who IS the killer?"

The question seemed to unnerve the butler, but thankfully, he didn't break into dance. Instead, he answered by saying,

"I don't know, sir. I wouldn't want to say I could be so far off, but I've always heard that a knife is a woman's weapon of choice. Give a man a gun any day, and he'll know what to do. Women don't trust the mechanics of a gun. Afraid it'll backfire and end up shooting themselves."

Reginald lowered his voice…"And I noticed, Detective, you didn't ask why I was tap dancing. Thank you for that. I've been that way since I was a child. Nervous habit."

With that, Reginald Carter clicked his heels and left the room. Tracy looked after him.

Was the butler the key to solving this crime? Did he know more than he was saying? Was he lying when he said he left John Roth in the library? Did he see Roth return to the house?

Tracy filed these thoughts away and made a minor entry in his notebook: **Butler, Reginald Carter thinks a woman committed the crime. The knife is a woman's weapon. P.S. He isn't a bad dancer.**

* * *

"Whoever killed him was counting on one thing...all skeletons look alike."
-The Thin Man (1934)

The sixteen people were sitting perfectly still in the circle of chairs when Tracy re-entered the room. The butler had already taken his seat. The detective looked from one to another.

"Alright, everyone, Reginald provided me a layout of the events that unfolded the night before you arrived at the party. Based on police records and the initial investigation, I clearly understand what transpired here on December 17th of last year. You were all present; no one left early or arrived late. Nobody seemed to wander around upstairs, and the party remained confined to the downstairs area. However, I need to clarify a few things, starting with why Mr. Roth wasn't at the party and why no one questioned his absence."

"I can answer that, Detective." A voice offered from the left side of Tracy's shoulder. It was the current Mrs. Roth, Beatrice Pearson Roth, or as everyone called her, Bitsy. Dolled up in her pale mink coat, the deceased's wife wasn't exactly the picture of a grieving widow. Of course, up until four days ago, she had only been the poor woman whose husband had been missing for a year. This widow thing was a new role for Bitsy, and she hadn't laid out the ground rules.

"The truth, Detective Tracy, is that my husband, rather my late husband, was NOT expected at the party that night. He didn't feel well. He suffered from severe migraines. When he left the house that day, he told me he was attending the country club. When he didn't come home, I assumed he must still be there taking a steam. That always seemed to relieve his headaches. So, I got dressed and went to the Howells' party alone."

A man to Detective Tracy's right spoke up. It was Drake Carrington. "She's right, Detective. J.R. came to the club. I saw him there myself. We grabbed a drink. Martinis. He told me he was skipping the party and going home to bed. We parted ways, and that was that. I didn't expect to see him at the party."

"How long were you with him, Mr. Carrington?"

"Oh, forty-five minutes, give or take a minute or two. I was dressing for the party at the club and meeting my wife here. I kept track of the time to prevent my being late."

"And you never saw him after he left the club?" Drake Carrington shook his head in the negative. Tracy turned back to the assembled. "Okay, folks. As I may have mentioned, I'm on loan to the South Hampton Police Department from the 19th Precinct in Manhattan and will be working on the case. I will need to speak with a few of you privately and briefly. So, Mrs. Roth, please follow me into the kitchen."

* * *

"You know how to whistle, don't you? Just put your lips together and blow."
-To Have and Have Not (1945)

The minute John Roth's widow slinked into the room, Tracy felt he needed to do his famous Bogey imitation, which always cracked up the guys at the station. Tracy noticed that Bitsy Roth resembled the love of Bogey's life, Lauren Bacall. Maybe it was the auburn wig and sultry bedroom eyes or the face- what a face: red lips, creamy foundation, and drawn-on eyebrows. It's a bit overdone, but who cared? She owned it.

"What time did you leave for the party, Mrs. Roth? And why didn't you find it strange that your husband had not returned home before you left?"

"Why should he hurry home to an empty house, Detective? Besides, this cocktail waitress at the club enjoyed draping herself around him, pretending he was the most interesting man ever."

"And was your husband right-handed or left-handed?"

"I'm not sure how that relates to anything, but he was left-handed, Detective."

"What about his taste in music?"

"Once again, I don't know the difference, but believe it or not, he liked country/western music."

"Do you know what was in the note that your husband delivered to Mr. Howell? What was so important that he had to come in person when a phone call would have been sufficient?"

Bitsy Roth smiled for the first time. "I apologize, Detective. J.R. never mentioned that he was coming to deliver anything to James. Perhaps he didn't call because he knew the Howells were en route to the party."

"Off the record, between you and me, Mrs. Roth, did anyone out there wish your husband dead?"

Bitsy Roth stared at Tracy. The smile disappeared from her red lips. "No, Detective. I don't believe any of these individuals are capable of murder. It must have been someone from the Howell staff or an intruder. A stranger. Is that possible? I think it is."

"Possible but not probable. Thank you for your candor, Mrs. Roth. Could you ask Mr. Howell to step in?"

Bitsy Roth tossed her hair back, squared her shoulders, and sashayed to the connecting door. Before passing through, she glanced back and shared some information with Tracy regarding her husband's migraine prescription. Mr. Roth's reaction to his medicine aligned with what Reginald, the butler, had informed him: no driving while on medication.

Tracy watched after Bitsy Roth for a moment and then quickly added a second line to the bottom of his notebook: ***John Roth, left-handed, liked country music. Bitsy Roth, the victim's wife, suggested a member of the Howell staff could be the killer. Or an outside intruder. What staff member would have a motive? Outside intruder, is that possible? Were the doors secure? Too late to find out.***

* * *

"And I always choke on that silver spoon."
-Citizen Kane (1941)

James Howell III entered his kitchen, looking around with a tinge of nostalgia in his eyes. Judging by his size, Tracy wondered if this might be James Howell's favorite room in the old house. Were there late-night pantry raids when everyone upstairs was asleep? The staff would discover remnants of his scavenging in the morning. In his mind, Detective Tracy had already assigned a character to James Howell. He had heard that this large, rotund man was rich, eccentric, elusive, yet hovering on the edge of genius—someone larger than life in stature and character—perhaps Orson Welles posing as Charles Foster Kane.

"Okay, I'm here, Detective. So, what can I do for you?"

"Just a few questions, Mr. Howell. I'm sure you want to discover your friend's killer. Perhaps you can tell me who knew about that secret closet in your library?"

"Everyone, Detective. There was nothing secret about it. At one time or another, every person out there has opened that panel and looked inside. I wish we had opened it that night."

Tracy pulled out the notes from the original investigation. They contained everyone's statement. He continued, "About the note the deceased delivered before the party, your butler was sure he saw it on the desk. You claimed here in your original statement that you never saw a note. What might have been in that note? You've had a year to think about it."

"I'm only speculating here, Detective, but I believe it may be related to a land deal that J.R. and I were working on. However, I can't explain why he wouldn't just pick up the phone and call me."

"And what do you think happened to the note? Since you never saw it, someone removed the note before you came into the library."

"No one would be interested in some note that J.R. wrote to me. How boring and unimportant."

"Unless it wasn't. Unimportant, that is." James Howell sniffed loudly as if dismissing any further inquiries regarding the note.

"Okay, Mr. Howell. Just one last question. Off the record. Who among your guests that night had a reason to kill Mr. Roth? Is there anyone with a solid motive?"

"I have no idea, but I want you to find out. My house was used for a murder. It's not a good legacy for the old girl, and I'm sorry I snapped at you earlier, Detective. I'm a bit on edge. Recovering from this shock. To think the man was in that closet, dead, for a year is unnerving, to say the least. And I have Mrs. Howell to consider."

A random thought suddenly passed through Tracy's mind. "Was it common knowledge that the house would be emptied, Mr. Howell?"

"Yes. Everyone understood that the house would remain empty for a few weeks. We ultimately decided to postpone the renovation. Constance and I would stay in the city. Everyone was aware."

"Okay. Thank you, sir. I may have some questions later."

James Howell nodded his understanding. However, he had something on his mind. "Will you need to question my wife, Detective? Constance is a bit delicate. Scares easily. She is quite upset by all this. I don't want her bothered."

James Howell compulsively closed the cupboards and drawers without waiting for an answer.

"As for your earlier question, Detective, I know it couldn't have been a member of my staff. They have all been loyal employees for years. And of the remaining party guests, you can eliminate the women. They would not have the strength to struggle with and overpower a man the size of J.R. And beyond those observances, I haven't even an educated guest."

"Okay, sir," Tracy replied. "If you would be so kind as to send in your server, Miss Penelope." As the mansion's owner pulled the cashmere overcoat around his ample girth and left the kitchen, Tracy made an additional entry: *James Howell, the host, insists no staff member is guilty. Why is he so sure? He also insists that no woman has the strength to wrestle with John Roth. On this point, he is probably right.*

* * *

"Murder sometimes smells like honeysuckle."
-Double Indemnity (1944)

Detective Tracy observed the Howells' serving girl pacing back and forth like a caged tiger. Miss Penelope's hands were in constant motion, touching her hair, face, and arms.

"I don't remember much, Detective. It's been over a year."

"I realize that, Miss Penelope. Let me know what you DO remember. Could you take this piece of paper and draw me a seating chart for the dining room table where everyone was seated?"

Penelope Smith stopped pacing for a moment. She grabbed the paper and drew the table and the fourteen chairs. She put a name on each place and handed it back to Tracy.

"Miss Penelope, when did you last see the deceased Mr. Roth?"

"The only time I saw Mr. Roth that night was when I let him out the door. I realize I was the last person to see him alive, which makes me nervous. I can assure you I didn't kill anybody."

"I'm sure you didn't, Miss Penelope. You say Mr. Roth went out the front door and down the steps to the waiting cab. Did you watch the cab drive away?"

"No, I did not. Mr. Roth was still walking when I closed the door, as I was asked to. I went into the dining room to check the place settings. Through the window I saw the cab."

"Could you see Mr. Roth in the backseat?"

"It was dark. I couldn't see inside the cab."

"Okay, Miss, that will be all for now."

"For now?" Miss Penelope asked.

"Yes, I may have some questions later." Before Penelope could escape, Tracy asked casually, without looking up from his pad…"Off the record, Miss, could you offer a guess as to who you think may have committed this murder? No pressure, you don't have to answer. I was just curious. You seem like an observant young woman."

Penelope Smith shook her head as she hugged her arm around her torso. "Detective, I wouldn't want to be accused of being a snitch or anything, but for as many parties as I have seen in this house and as many times as I have waited on these people, the one person I've never trusted is Zuzu Gabbard."

"Maybe you could explain yourself a little clearer."

"Well, since it's off the record, whenever I have served at the Howell's parties, that La-De-Da woman would pull me out and ask me to put her next to this or that gentleman. Ask me to change the place cards to suit her fancy. And if I didn't do what she asked, she would run me ragged the rest of the night, sending me for drinks and trumped-up things she didn't need. If you ask me, she is big trouble. I don't have any proof; I didn't catch her with a knife or anything like that."

"And did Miss Gabbard ask you to switch the place cards the night of December 17th last year?"

"I honestly don't remember, sir. I think they got switched. They looked different when I returned to the dining room after all the guests had arrived. But it wasn't me that did the switching."

"Anything else you can add, Miss Penelope?"

"Yes... I don't like to talk ill of anyone, especially the dead, but I think the dinner party that night was haunted. As soon as we knew Mr. Roth was not attending and I removed his place card, it was as if someone was walking on his grave. Like everyone out there knew he was going to die. And on top of all that, thirteen for dinner is a very unlucky number. I would never have gone through with it."

Penelope Smith crossed herself quickly and turned towards the door. When she left the room, Detective Tracy stared at the drawing she had made of the seating arrangement.

	James Howell III	
D. Crawley		B. Roth (Door to kitchen)
D. Winston		L. Winthorpe
T. Carlisle	*Dining*	J. VanHouten
C. Carrington	*Room*	D. Thielberg
R. Crawley	*Table*	Z. Gabbard
(Empty seat)		D. Carrington (Door to Library)
	Constance Howell	

Detective Tracy folded the paper and stuffed it in his pocket; it might come in handy. Then he added another line to his little notebook:
Miss Penelope, the server, thinks Zuzu Gabbard is capable of murder. The designer may have switched the place cards to put her next to someone. Who would she want to be seated next to? And why?

* * *

"Made it, Ma, top of the world."
-White Heat (1949)

Detective Tracy had purposely not sent Miss Penelope in search of another guest, so he was surprised when Mr. Theodore Carlisle stuck his head through the kitchen door and gave a whistle. "Can I see you a moment, Detective?" (Oh boy, this one was easy. James Cagney in every movie they had ever made. That was Ted Carlisle.)

"Certainly, sir. Step in."

James Howell's best friend and confidante closed the door behind himself. He was of medium height and weight, but his face was full of character. Any woman in the room would say he was attractive, a dash of scoundrel and swagger. "I don't want to talk out of school, Detective. I didn't know much about John Roth, but I'd seen him at a few of Jim's parties and even played poker with him in this house. When you've played poker with a man, you find out what he's made of. So, from those few observations, I deduced that the man was slightly shady. I wouldn't have trusted him with any land deals, but my friend, Jim Howell, is smart, and when he talks, other smart people listen. I've kept my mouth shut. I just have a gut feeling, Detective. You never really know what people are thinking. They say one thing but mean another. No one out there has love lost for the late Mr. Roth. Do you see my point?"

"No, sir. I'm not sure I do," Tracy stated. (The detective had a feeling Carlisle was about to make him see.)

"Well, it's like this, Detective. You are never going to know who did it. Everyone had a dislike for the man. As far as I can see, anyone could have killed the old boy. Not the women, of course. And even though I know you look at the spouse first, Bitsy Roth certainly had nothing to do with her husband's death. So, what can come of all this investigating stuff? The case is colder than a doorknob in winter. I know you must go through the formalities, but I'm afraid you are wasting your time."

"It's my time to waste, Mr. Carlisle, And in the past, cold cases have been solved. It's just a matter of digging deeper than your predecessors, and I was wondering, sir, what sort of music do you listen to?"

Theodore Carlisle's trench coat fell away as he jammed his hands into the pockets with surprise. "I don't know, Detective. I can't say that I listen to much of anything. I will occasionally turn on the oldies, as the kids say these days. Perhaps something from the '40s. If you have any more questions, feel free to ask."

"Okay, sir. As they say at the felt tables, I've been dealt a tough hand. Who do you think is the killer?"

Theodore Carlisle chuckled—a nervous laugh. "Is that your poker face? Did I give the impression that I know something? I'm sorry if I did because I don't. But if I were betting on this hand, I would exclude the women, including the wife. Any man who isn't blind can see that Bitsy is above reproach. So, I look for the man with the most to lose. Whoever committed this murder thought it out in advance. Now, will there be anything else?"

"Nothing right now, Mr. Carlisle. Unless, of course, you saw or heard something the night of the party. Or you saw Mr. Roth return to the mansion. I think we're done. Could you please send in Mr. Carrington?"

Theodore Carlisle nodded a quick goodbye and smiled, Cagney style. He turned for the door. When he was gone, Tracy made another entry in his book: **Theodore Carlisle, a friend of James Howell, excludes women. He says Bitsy Roth would never commit such a crime. He points to men with business losses. Who falls into that category? Everyone.**

* * *

"Hey, what hit me?" "That last martini, darling..."
-The Thin Man (1934)

The minute Drake Carrington's long legs strolled casually through the kitchen door, Tracy thought of William Powell in the Thin Man series. He was tall, suave, sophisticated, ascot-wearing, and confident. He didn't mince words and got right down to business, just as the Thin Man would have done.

"You wanted to see me, Detective? Here I am."

"Yes, Mr. Carrington. You mentioned earlier that you were at the country club with Mr. Roth on the night in question. Did he say anything about going to the Howell residence when he left?"

"No, he didn't."

"Did you notice his car in the club parking lot when you left? How much time had passed?"

"After John left me, I went to the locker room and dressed for the party. I would say maybe ten minutes or so had elapsed. And when I went out to my car, it was dark, and I never noticed the Bentley. Before you ask, I don't know why Mr. Roth took a cab here to the Howells."

"About the car, I'm sure you've heard the police found it parked in the back lot the next day."

"Yes, Detective, I have heard." Drake Carrington's thin little pencil mustache began to twitch. Tracy waited for the twitching to stop before proceeding.

"Now, sir, did Mr. Roth say anything about needing to see James Howell about anything?"

"No, he didn't. He never mentioned Jim the entire time I was with him."

"Do you think he was concerned about anything in his personal or business life?"

"No. We discussed sports, the stock market, and the usual topics. Perhaps a word or two about our wives, but that was it."

Tracy felt as if he were getting nowhere with the Thin Man. He was offering no new information. "Okay, Mr. Carrington. That's all for now. I may have a few questions later." As the land baron left the room, Tracy asked his usual question. Carrington's back was to him; he couldn't gauge his reaction. But there was little doubt that nothing could break that ice-cold exterior. "Off the record, Mr. Carrington, do you have any suspicions? Just between us, man to man."

Carrington turned slowly. The mustache twitch was back. "I have a few theories, Detective, but I feel reluctant to say. But if this is off, and I mean WAY off the record, I will tell you what I think." Carrington seemed to pause before delivering what he believed was a betrayal. "J.R. comes here to see Jim. He leaves a note on the desk. Jim reads the note and then destroys it. Afterward, J.R. returns to the house following the party and confronts Jim. They argue, and that's when Jim kills him. This might explain why the construction was delayed for so long- giving the body time to decompose in that secret closet. Of course, this is merely pure conjecture."

Tracy stood. He hadn't expected such an elaborate and well-thought-out explanation. The man was good. But what else would you expect from the Thin Man? "Okay, Mr. Carrington. As you say, it's just a theory."

"Well, Detective, we have all had a year to think. I knew J.R. wouldn't just leave the country without his money. Foul play was always the guess of everyone in that hall, whether they admit it or not." With another twitch of his mustache, Carrington left the room. Detective Tracy smiled for the first time that night as he wrote in his notebook: ***Drake Carrington believes that James Howell is the guilty one. Did John Roth return to the mansion sometime after the party? If so, why not drive his car? What was in the note?***

* * *

"I distrust a closed mouth man.
Generally, he picks the wrong time to talk."
-The Maltese Falcon (1941)

Detective Tracy strode from the kitchen, returning to the great hall. Everyone was now milling about, talking among themselves. The length of time had loosened the tension. A hush fell over the room as he entered and moved to the center of the semicircle.

"Okay, I have spoken with everyone who had contact with Mr. Roth the day and night of his disappearance. I will be calling on a few of you. I want one more meeting here in the great hall. Perhaps a week from now." Tracy paused for effect. Then continued, "I won't lie to you. This is a very cold case. A year ago, Mr. Roth walked out of this house and never returned, only to be found in one of the empty closets a year later. I have taken the time to read your statements and examine the crime scene photographs, which included the inside of Mr. Roth's car."

"What happens, Detective, if you can't come to any conclusions?" It was Bitsy Roth who spoke.

"My notes will go into your husband's overstuffed file; then it will get shoved into the cold case room where someone will drag it out someday and waste the taxpayer's money." Bitsy nodded knowingly. Everyone did. "Until we meet, please don't leave town. Don't speak to anyone regarding the case, and please, whatever you do, don't take interviews from the press or television stations."

Douglas Winston, an insanely wealthy man-about-town, spoke... "Do we need to consult our lawyers, Detective?"

"Only if you feel you need one, Mr. Winston." The millionaire stared at Tracy without flinching as the detective turned to his room full of suspects. "Everyone is free to go. But please stop in the kitchen. Laid out are papers with everyone's name, address, and telephone number. Make sure that all information on those papers is correct."

The partygoers shuffled into the construction-worn kitchen, eyeing Detective Tracy as they moved. Once everyone had left, Tracy sat down on the nearest crate. He failed to notice the footsteps behind him. A voice startled him out of his random thoughts. "Excuse me, Detective. I wondered if you completely agreed my wife wouldn't be questioned. Is it necessary to have her return next week? Right now, this house unnerves her."

Tracy addressed James Howell straight on... "I'm very sorry, Mr. Howell, but I need Mrs. Howell to be present next week."

"Okay, Detective. I don't like your answer, but I'll follow your instructions. So, until then." With that, the mansion owner left the room. Maybe Drake Carrington was correct. James Howell's request to keep his wife out of the interrogation line seemed urgent. Why was that exactly? Did

Constance Howell know something that the others didn't? Did she see something? Detective Tracy crossed the great hall and out the front door. He had a feeling next week was going to come too soon. Or, in the case of the killer, maybe not soon enough.

* * *

"The perfect murder? Only on paper."
-Dial M for Murder (1954)

Detective Tracy rode the elevator to the top floor of the mid-Manhattan building, where Douglas Winston awaited him, standing at attention. "Cool" was the word that came to Tracy's mind, reminiscent of the ever-steady Mr. Ray Miland in the classic mystery Dial M for Murder. At 41, Winston was tall, thin, and prematurely gray. "Please come in, Detective Tracy."

And that's precisely what Tracy did, as both men sat across the table from one another. "A few questions, Mr. Winston. How were you acquainted with the deceased, Mr. Roth?"

"James Howell introduced us a few years ago. I thought we might be able to strike up some business deals. I met Bitsy Roth at a charity function; she was interesting, and I thought her husband might be as well. Then came the first bad deal. The last time I saw him, he crossed the street to avoid me."

"Did you see Mr. Roth the night of the party? Before or after the other guests had arrived?"

"No. I heard J.R. was not attending the Howell's party, so I didn't expect to see him."

"Ok, Mr. Winston. You wouldn't have much of a reason to kill the man, so who do you think did?"

"Over the last 12 months, I've developed a few ideas, but every road has always led back to one person—his wife. Bitsy is obsessed with money, and Mr. Roth is about to go bankrupt. She had to eliminate him. A rich widow sounded much more appealing than a broke ex-wife."

"Well, for someone who liked Bitsy when they met her, you seem to have changed your tune. Which reminds me: what sort of music do you prefer to listen to?"

"Classical, if you must know. And as far as Bitsy goes, I didn't say I liked her. I said she was very interesting. And murder is always interesting. Don't you agree?"

Tracy gathered up his notebook and then spoke, "I think that's all for today."

Douglas Winston stood before delivering a parting shot. "Just remember one thing, Detective. Everyone has spent the last year talking and comparing notes. And sometimes talk breeds changes."

Later, Tracy would add another line to his notebook: ***Douglas Winston is sure Bitsy Roth plunged the knife into her husband. If she did, is it possible that someone helped her? Someone at the table that night? What motive would Bitsy Roth have for killing her husband? Possible bankruptcy, life insurance?***

* * *

*"I'm busy seeing that you don't
lose any of that money I married you for."
-The Thin Man (1934)*

Dressed to kill, Drake Carrington's wife sauntered through the local precinct. She demanded to see Detective Tracy. No, she didn't have an appointment; she was confident he would see her. As Christy Carrington walked down the hall, introductions were unnecessary. She was the perfect Myrna Loy to her husband, William Powell.

"Please have a seat, Mrs. Carrington. Can I offer you some water?" Tracy stated.

Christy Carrington removed her dark glasses. She was attractive with or without the shades. Tracy was expecting sassy, snappy answers. And he wasn't disappointed. "No, I won't be staying long, Detective," answering with narrowing eyes that looked about. "Not as impressive as I was expecting."

Tracy countered. "I'm sorry to disappoint you. Don't go in much for decorating."

"Who said I was talking about the office, Detective?" (Tracy almost laughed out loud. There was an insult in there somewhere.)

"I'm sorry I missed your little dog and pony show at the Howell's mansion the other day, Detective Tracy. But I'm here. Let's get this over with. I have a nail appointment." "Ok, Mrs. Carrington, I just wanted to ask how well you knew Mr. Roth. And your general impression?"

"I knew J.R. only through occasional social encounters, and my overall impression of him was not favorable. His wife, Bitsy, married him for his money. I recognized all the signs because I did the same. I snagged Drake for his name and that hefty bank account. He knows it, and so does everyone else. I'm trying to persuade him to keep as much as possible."

"I see. And are those losses attributed to Mr. Roth and his business deals?"

"Yes. And, of course, there's Drake's gambling problem. Horses mainly. And occasional stops in Atlantic City. He does love the dice. But he's not the only one."

"And to whom are you referring, Mrs. Carrington?"

"Please call me Christy, Detective, and I'm referring to Richard Crawley, of course."

"Of course."

"I've seen Richard pick the daily double at Belmont and toss it all away on the next race. And he and Drake can't wait to get to the craps table the minute our plane lands in Jersey. Drake and Richard have the same affliction, and there is no cure. So, they need money, lots of it. Richard Crawley has more money than God Himself, and Drake can't keep up. But he does try."

"Okay, just one more question, ma'am. If you were to bet, like your husband, who would you put your money on in this investigation?

"I don't know. I have a few random thoughts. Why didn't someone check the Howell's mansion sooner? Why didn't Bitsy hire a private investigator to look for J.R.? We all knew he didn't just pick up and move away without all his money and precious car. He loved that Bentley."

"What are you saying, Mrs. Carrington? That no one cared enough? And who would that point to?"

"Why not his best friend, Lawrence Winthorpe? Don't let that shiny wheelchair fool you, Detective. The man walks when he wants to. Lawrence Winthorpe was JR's financial advisor because he knew where all the skeletons were buried- forgive the pun. Lawrence did not bother to try to find JR. Why? Because he knew the man was dead."

"Ok, Mrs. Carrington, you can go now. Please don't speak to anyone regarding the case. I'm sorry, I have one more question. What sort of music does your husband prefer?"

"What a strange question. Drake is adamant about opera. He listens to it day and night, dragging me, kicking and screaming to the performances. He is even on board of the New York Opera Society."

"Okay, thank you, Christy, for coming in. You may go." Christy Carrington nodded and left the office. Her stiletto heels could be heard clicking on the cold linoleum as she exited the station. Detective, Rudy Myers, stuck his head into Tracy's office. He couldn't help but ask…

"Who the hell was that good-looking wool? And why do you get all the cases that involve good-looking women?" Tracy threw a pencil at Myers and pulled out his notebook. He made a new entry at the bottom*: **Christie Carrington believes that Lawrence Winthorpe, a financial advisor, is*** *the prime suspect. Winthorpe did not organize a search party. Who stood to benefit from JR's death, besides his wife? Winthorpe?*

* * *

*"Stealing a man's wife, that's nothing.
But stealing his car."
-The Postman Always Rings Twice (1946)*

The maid answered Tracy's third knock at the Lawrence Winthorpe residence, a lovely fancy house on the island not far from the Howell's mansion. She showed Tracy to a large living room with tapestry drapes and comfy sofas. The detective took a seat in a small wing-back chair and waited. He heard the squeak of the wheels before he saw the man. Lawrence Winthorpe entered the room, paused, and then adjusted the steel chair to face the detective. He rested his hands across his lap, an Ironside move that recalls Raymond Burr in his second most iconic role.

"Detective, it's nice to see you again. I assume you're here to ask me a few questions. I was wondering when you were going to get around to me."

"Mr. Winthorpe, I understand you were a very good friend of John Roth's and his financial advisor. Someone even referred to you as Roth's buddy. Is that a fair statement?"

"Yes, Detective, it is. I was J.R.'s friend, and I advised him whenever he asked. Not that he always listened to my advice. J.R. was his own man. I miss him."

"Funny. But you are the first person to say that. I saw the Bentley in the driveway when I drove up. I'm guessing it was Mr. Roth's."

"Yes, Detective. Bitsy gave me the Bentley a few months ago when she assumed J.R. was never coming home. She didn't want it to sit idle. She doesn't drive. Neither do I."

"You don't have to explain, Mr. Winthrope. Just give me a fair assessment of Mr. Roth, in your opinion.

"Detective J.R. was stuck in time between age 12 and 14."

"Most men are," said Tracy.

"And he was a scoundrel. He did things like lose other people's money along with his own. It was his weakness. No one is going to sing his praises. I liked him, but very few did."

"You write his obituary?"

"Yes. How did you guess?" Lawrence Winthorpe chuckled; his boyish haircut flopped over his steady brown eyes.

"Too much honesty is never a good thing, Detective."

"No, sir. It's not. And now, just one more off-the-record question. Who and why?"

Winthorpe got up from the wheelchair and walked slowly to the window facing his massive lawn before answering. "Zuzu Gabbard hated J.R. She wanted Bitsy Roth all to herself. Lunches, shopping, the theater, that's Zuzu's world when she's not designing her high-end clothing line. And Zuzu likes Bitsy's company. J.R was always getting in the way. So, Zuzu killed him. Not that I have proof."

"Did you see Mr. Roth return to the mansion that night? And how did Ms. Gabbard pull this off?"

"No, I didn't see J.R. return to the Howell's. And I don't want to put ideas in your head, Detective. Let's say that Zuzu knew about the secret closet; we all did. Reginald told me she was the first guest at the party that night. Perhaps J.R was there in the library. The house was going to be empty for at least six months. She took a chance. She thought she got away with it until a few days ago."

"Very neat little theory, Mr. Winthorpe. How do you think Ms. Gabbard lifted Mr. Roth into the secret closet? She couldn't have done it alone. Who helped her?" Tracy watched as the financial advisor returned to his iron chair. He sat down hard.

"You must find these answers yourself, Detective Tracy. I'm going upstairs now for a rest. Please see yourself out. I may have said too much, but I hope I've been helpful."

Lawrence Winthorpe rolled out of the room and through an open elevator door. The elevator closed and ascended while Detective Tracy wrote in his notebook. Suddenly, he could hear the sounds of early rock'n'roll playing upstairs. When the maid came to let him out, he was still writing as he addressed her.

"Mr. Winthorpe listens to Elvis?"

The large woman with a head full of curls smiled and nodded her head in the affirmative. "Yes, sir. He is the King, after all. I'm speaking of Elvis, of course."

Tracy continued to write in his notebook: **Lawrence Winthorpe says Zuzu Gabbard committed the crime but has no explanation of how she got him in the closet. If she had help, who would be the most likely candidate? Reginald the Butler? James Howell, the homeowner? Or the next person to arrive that night? P.S. Winthorpe has the Bently.**

* * *

"A man doesn't tell a woman what to do.
She tells herself."
-Notorious (1946)

Like Christy Carrington, Zuzu Gabbard entered the police station without an appointment. She asked about Detective Tracy's availability and sat on a nearby bench without waiting to be invited. When Tracy entered the holding area, Miss Gabbard seemed to be humming a tune.

"Is that a love song, Miss Gabbard?"

"Love song, Detective? Really? There's nothing like a love song to give you a good laugh."

Did she model herself after the stunning actress with those liquid brown eyes? Her chin-length dark hair was casually draped around her face, and her outfit was tasteful and elegant. Tracy nearly bit his tongue when she quoted Ingrid Bergman. Tracy guessed that if he could see inside that suit collar, he would find her couture label. The designer rose and followed the detective down the hallway to his office. Tracy held a preconceived notion of Zuzu Gabbard's personality, but Zuzu was about to prove him wrong.

"I wanted to know if I could help, Detective. What piece of the puzzle are you missing?"

"*Who* killed John Roth."

Zuzu Gabbard laughed out loud. "That's a big piece of the puzzle, Detective. Give me something smaller to start with."

"How about this? There's a rumor among the Howell staff that you changed the place cards at the party that night. Did you ask someone to change the place cards the night of the party last December?"

"No, Detective. Someone did it before I could. When we went into dinner, something was different."

Tracy turned around to consult the crude seating chart Miss Penelope had drawn. It was thumb-tacked to the corkboard on the wall behind his desk. "You were between Mr. Thielberg and Mr. Carrington. Which one did the switching?"

"That's not a nice thing to ask a lady, Detective. I could lie. So, I will say Devin Thielberg."

"Is that a lie?"

"No."

"And is THAT a lie, Miss Gabbard?"

"Yes. No. Which would you like it to be, Detective? If you want facts, I remember a switch with the place cards. Maybe someone wanted to sit by me. Flattering, unless it was the killer. To be safe, I've erased everyone's names from my little black book. Even if they buy my dresses."

"Can you tell me anything about that night? Was there anything unusual?"

"Nothing. I'm sorry. Other than the fact that J.R was missing from the table."

"Did anyone leave the table during dinner? Did anyone go into the library, Miss Gabbard?"

"Penelope and the butler, Reginald, came in or out through the dining room door."

"Assuming there is a murder, who do you think committed this crime, Miss Gabbard?"

"If I had to make an educated guess, I would say Bitsy Roth killed her husband. Shocking, I know. She is a good friend and one of my best clients. But isn't it always the first place you look, the wife with a bad taste in her mouth? I always say if all else fails, look to the heart."

"Would it interest you to know, Miss Gabbard, that one of the guests at the table that night thinks you are the killer? Your motive, the continued companionship of Bitsy Roth."

Zuzu Gabbard laughed out loud. "That came from Lawrence Winthorpe. He is still upset about the time I sent him and J.R. on a wild goose chase."

"Miss Gabbard, that's all my questions today. You are free, but please ensure you are at the mansion next week. I need everyone to be there. I hope to have answers, but I can't promise anything. This is a very cold case."

With that, Zuzu Gabbard left the office. Tracy watched as she walked down the corridor and out the station's door into the street. He grabbed his notebook and made an entry: ***Zuzu Gabbard thinks Bitsy Roth killed her husband. Did Bitsy Roth confide in her? And who rats on their best friend? A killer.***

* * *
"Don't you need a coat?"
"No, you will do."
-Sorry, Wrong Number (1946)

    Stepping into the spider's web, Detective Tracy had no idea what he was in for. Outside Jacqueline VanHouten's building, Detective Tracy engaged with the button by the front door. Soon, he was buzzed into apartment number one, where the jet-setting socialite opened the door to greet him. The apartment was lavish yet tasteful; the same could be said for its owner. Jacqueline VanHouten was tall, long-legged, and perfect in both face and form- a classic beauty with proportionate features. Her thick blonde hair fell across her shoulders in deep waves, cascading over the silk dressing gown the color of the blush wallpaper. In her 50s, she seemed to defy time and gravity. "I won't keep you long, Miss VanHousten. Just a few questions," the detective specified.

    "I'll bet you say that to all the girls." The socialite said with a smile. "Please have a seat. It's the maid's day off. We are alone. Does that make you nervous? I promise I won't bite, at least not too hard."

    Tracy shook off the chemistry brewing between them and got back to business. "I would like to ask you, Miss VanHouten, about your relationship with Mr. Roth. Was he your friend?"

    "Friend is not the word I would use. It's impossible to be friends with a man. They always want something. It's a cat and mouse game, and sometimes I'm the cat."

    "So, your relationship with Mr. Roth was strictly social in a group setting?"

    "I didn't say that, Detective."

    "Well then, what are you saying, Miss VanHouten?"

    "A girl never tells. Unless, of course, she wants trouble."

"Trouble? Are you saying you know who killed him, Miss VanHouten?" The question seemed to disquiet the jet-setting socialite. But only momentarily.

"I'm not sure, Detective. I have suspicions like everyone else. It had to be someone at the party that night because the house was locked tighter than a drum after the last guest left. But how do you narrow down the suspects? Who can you eliminate? I wouldn't put this past either of the Crawleys. I say it's a crime of passion. J.R. could be charming if he wanted to be."

Tracy couldn't help himself; he was fascinated. She was good. For the first time, he couldn't put an old movie star with the charming Miss VanHouten. Marilyn Monroe? Jean Harlow? Veronica Lake? No. None of those. Jacqueline VanHouten showed Tracy to the door. Without a word, she watched as he left. Out in the foyer, Tracy opened his notebook and added another line: ***Jacqueline VanHouten thinks of crime as passion. She mentioned the Crawleys. Interesting. ..reason?***

* * *

"A successful man is one who makes more money than his wife can spend."
-Lana Turner (1955)

The Crawleys were home, waiting for Detective Tracy's arrival. The detective found the husband and wife sitting side by side, holding hands. Dora Crawley's legs were bare and crossed, reminiscent of Lana Turner's signature move in 'The Postman Always Rings Twice.' A seething gesture that spoke volumes. Richard Crawley pulled on his ear nervously. Dora had a British accent, but Richard had a British demeanor. "Good of you to come, Tracy. I hope we can answer some of your questions."

"I hope you can answer ALL of them, Mr. Crawley."

"Yes, of course, what I meant." Richard Crawley indicated an overstuffed chair located nearby. Tracy sat down as if being ordered.

"Let's start with your relationship with Mr. Roth. Were you friends, or did you have some business dealings with him over the years?"

"We had a few investments with J.R. They weren't always lucrative; most did not pan out, but he kept trying to get us to continue our relationship beyond the social bounds." Dora Crawley disentangled her hand from her husband's. That was a sign to Tracy.

"We don't care much for either of the Roths, Detective. He was crass, not kosher. And she, well, Bitsy is a snob. They fought regularly; it was exhausting being around them. But on certain social occasions, they couldn't be avoided. We moved in the same circles as the Roths."

Detective Tracy turned to Dora. The wife's eyes had never strayed from his face. "Mrs. Crawley, did you see Mr. Roth return from the mansion the night of the party?"

"I didn't see J.R. at all that night. Returning or otherwise. And as far as the guests go, Bitsy isn't all that bad. She's a bit trying at times, but that's all. Now, Constance Howell, that's a whole different story. All the men think she's an idiot, but she likes it that way. It puts up a shield, so she's never expected to be an expert on any subject. And it gives her an excuse to keep quiet. She observes."

"Okay, do either of you know Mr. Roth's enemies?" Both Crawleys shook their heads in the negatives. "Well, if you hear anything in the future, please let me know."

"Of course," replied Richard Crawley. "We want to cooperate fully. Help you in any way we can."

"One final question for both of you, off the record. Who do you believe killed Mr. Roth?"

The Crawleys turned to one another at precisely the same time. Dora Crawley was the spokesman. "We have discussed that very thing, Detective. Richard and I both agree that Oliver Winston is the most likely IF it's a murder. Not for anything, but we have heard that he lost much money last year."

"Do you believe Mr. Winston is capable of murder? And how could he have pulled it off?"

"Oh yes, Oliver is very capable of murder. He's a bit of a hot head but jumps at his own shadow. He's nice socially but has a devious mind, displayed several times. And don't you find that everyone can murder at one time or another?"

Tracy stood, making a final gesture. He didn't bother to confirm Dora Crawley's observation. "Thank you both for your candor. I will see you next week at the Howell's mansion. Please be careful not to speak to the press if they come around asking for interviews. I hope to have a suspect by next week."

The Crawleys stood sliding off the ventriloquist's knee. Richard shook his hand. Dora only smiled, like the caged canary who is examining the cat. When Tracy left, he added to his notebook: **The Crawleys suspect Oliver Winston. Why? Was something said that they didn't want to repeat? May it incriminate them? Could Winston be a murderer?**

* * *

*"If that knife is missing,
I'll look for it in your back."
-The Thin Man (1934)*

Detective Tracy saved Devin Thielberg for last. For several reasons. Thielberg had been an out-of-town guest the night of the party. Traveling from California, he stayed at a nearby hotel, but since then, he has returned to California. So, this interview was going to involve a phone call to Hollywood. Tracy didn't have much hope of getting additional information from Thielberg. And the element of surprise, the facial reaction to a question asked, would not be possible. Tracy wanted to make the call anyway. Tracy admired the director as a film enthusiast. Thielberg created modern movies, action thrillers, romantic stories, and children films. His work was remarkable. Tracy could envision Thielberg producing great films had he lived in the 1930s, 1940s, or 1950s. He would have been one of the great film directors of the time, giving them a run for the Oscar. Tracy dialed the number James Howell had given him and waited for an answer. He was finally connected after talking to several secretaries and an assistant.

"Hello, Detective Tracy. I understand from Jim that you have located our missing Mr. Roth. Sounds like a grisly little problem for someone. How can I help?"

"Just a few questions, sir. Did you know the deceased Mr. John Roth?"

"I didn't know him, Detective. I met most of those people for the first time the night of the dinner party, except, of course, the Howells and the Carrington's. James Howell and I had been friends in New York at earlier times. And I met both Carrington's about a year ago at a similar party. I'm in town during the holidays. It seems more like Christmas in the East. Here in L.A., they decorate palm trees, and good old Santa is stuffed into shorts and a Hawaiian shirt."

Detective Tracy chuckled. He had a vision. "As a director, I'm sure you are quite observant. Do you recall anything unusual from that night? Did anyone mention anything about the deceased not being at the party?"

"No, I don't think I heard the man's name mentioned. His wife was present, Betty or Betsy, or something like that. I met her briefly. She was very nice."

"During dinner, do you remember if anyone left the table for any reason?"

"No. I was sitting between Miss VanHouten and Miss Gabbard. I can attest that neither of them left the table during dinner. I would have had a break if they had."

Tracy paused and summoned up his courage. It was now or never. "I apologize, sir, but this is somewhat off the topic. Being in the film industry, you can appreciate what I'm about to share. Whenever I have a case, I assign old black-and-white film stars to my suspects. It's a game, yet it proves helpful."

"Interesting tactic, Detective. I hope you'll give me some leading men like Tyrone Power. But when it comes to the other men, let me guess. Perhaps a William Powell, a Bogart, a Cagney, an Eddie G., and a Fred MacMurray? Am I right?"

"I would have been disappointed if you hadn't been, sir. I would have to take you down from that pedestal I have you on—just two more things. First, everyone from the party will attend the Howell residence at the next meeting. I understand you can't make it. Secondly, could you please tell me who you would say was the killer if you were writing and directing this movie?"

Tracy listened as Thielberg cupped his hand over the phone receiver, shouted instructions to his secretary, and then returned to the line. He spoke at once. "Loaded question, Detective, but here it goes. I would resist the temptation to consider the most obvious suspect, the wife. Instead, I would look at one of the other attendees, someone who might harbor a grudge against Mr. Roth. But not an overtly obvious grudge. Perhaps Roth was being blackmailed. The killer would need time, so I would have Roth return to the house after everyone left the party. Then, when the killer confronted him, and the murder was committed, the body could easily have been moved into the closet. I would suggest no one would discover the body for months. Decomposition would be complete, providing more than enough time to dispose of the murder weapon, with no hope of coroner results on how he died." Thielberg paused as if for dramatics but continued. "Whoever committed this crime was resourceful. You have your hands full. I wish you luck, but unless you can uncover a motive, your chances of solving this murder are slim. I would hate to have to write the ending to this one, Detective. And even though you didn't ask me, I will be there next week. I wouldn't miss it for the world. I might get some ideas for my next screenplay."

And with that said, the line from California went dead. Tracy was already writing in his notebook: **Thielberg thinks there is a hidden motive. Blackmail? Eliminates Bitsy Ross and the staff. Depicts J.R. as a bad guy. But Thielberg is unfamiliar with the partygoers. Met them that night—pure conjecture. Big band music is playing in the background while on the phone.**

* * *

"Keep riding me, and
they'll be picking iron out of your liver."
-The Maltese Falcon (1941)

Detective Tracy spread his notes across the dining room table. While waiting for his TV dinner to cook, he planned to spend some time understanding the semantics of the Roth case. Tracy reviewed his timeline for each interview, including those conducted a year earlier by his predecessor, another detective.

- John Roth tells his wife he has a migraine and won't attend the dinner party.
- John Roth goes to the Country Club.
- Roth and Carrington have drinks at the bar.
- Roth leaves his car in the parking lot and takes a cab to Howell mansion, six blocks away.
- Roth arrives at the mansion. Reginald shows him into the library.

- Roth leaves a note on James Howell's desk.
- Reginald leaves Roth alone in the library and goes to the wine cellar cabinet.
- When Reginald returns, Roth is gone. Sees note on the desk.
- Penelope, the server, tells Reginald she let Roth out the front door.
- Penelope sees the cab leaving the driveway.
- Guests arrive.
- Zuzu Gabbard arrives first.
- Douglas Winston arrives last.
- No one goes upstairs to empty rooms.
- Penelope notices some place cards have been moved.
- After dinner, everyone leaves.
- Howells are the last to leave the house.
- Roth's car was discovered in the back parking lot of the country club the next day.
- The mansion has been closed and has not reopened for nearly a year.
- Upon the excavation, the victim is discovered wedged in a concealed closet. Everyone was aware of the closet.
- The kitchen opened into the dining room with double doors.
- The library opened into the kitchen and the dining room with double doors.
- The powder rooms on each side of the stairs opened into the Great Hall and the library.

When he finished the greasy bird, Tracy wiped his hands and mouth clean. An idea was forming in his mind. What if he looked at everyone's response to his question about the killer and motive and then assumed that they were lying? Could he make a case? Of course, he could. And there was one person on the list that made perfect sense. This person could have had a motive, created opportunity, and had accessibility. They fit with the 'choice of music.' This theory answered every question. Detective Tracy discarded the rest of his dinner and went to the phone. One thing was certain: what he believed was probable and the only logical explanation for what could have happened to Mr. John Roth on December 17, 1977.

* * *

> *"There is no terror in the bang,*
> *only in the anticipation of it."*
> *-A. Hitchcock (1956)*

    All were gathered in the Great Hall of Howells mansion, just as they had been that night. Devin Thielberg traveled from Los Angeles as he had said he would. Everyone was conversing among themselves as if they were at a peculiar party amidst the rubble of crumbling corridors from the past. Detective Tracy entered the room, accompanied by three law enforcement officers. Constance Howell was walking beside him. James Howell jumped up, and everyone fell silent as Constance sat beside her husband in one of the folding chairs. Her pale lips were pressed tightly together as though she could not speak. This was unexpected. Had Constance been questioned? Why? It seemed an arrest was forthcoming. Why else would the police officers be standing there, ready? But how could that be? No. No. Detective Tracy took his place inside the semicircle of chairs. He didn't mince words.

    "Good evening, everyone. I wonder if you would all please follow me to the dining room. The room has been cleared, and there are no hazards. Please bring the folding chair you are now sitting on. Thank you."

    Everyone shuffled into the vast dining room except for Lawrence Winthorpe, who rolled his wheelchair quietly.

Tracy placed an empty chair where John Roth would have sat had he been present. "I'm sure you've already guessed that I would ask you to set your chairs in the exact spot where you were the night of the party. Reginald and Penelope, please stand along the left side wall since you were not seated at the table." Reginald and Penelope complied with the request while everyone else moved about, finding their place just as they had the previous year. Lawrence Winthorpe rose from his wheelchair and sat in the chair James Howell had provided. Tracy stood in the center of the guests when everyone was in place. He took out his notebook and turned to the last page.

"This was a tough one, folks. Tough. I have a terrible habit of putting some of my favorite characters from the world of film on my suspects. This time, it was a mistake. I began to like you instead of suspecting you. The other mistake I made when this investigation started was placing too much importance on the note that John Roth left on Mr. Howell's desk before he was killed."

"But no note was found," James Howell interrupted from his chair at the head of the invisible table.

"I believe you, Mr. Howell. At first, I had several thoughts, until I spoke with Mrs. Howell this evening. She picked up the note when she saw it on the desk and forgot to give it to you. She told me she had read the note. It was nothing important, so she tossed it in the wastebasket. She was afraid to speak up, worried she was in trouble, so she asked you to keep me from questioning her for too long."

James Howell spoke once more. He had found his temper and then lost it just as quickly. "What is this nonsense, Detective? I feel as if I have landed in some bad movie. And I don't like it one bit."

"I'm sorry, Mr. Howell. Please be patient. I promise this won't take long. At least not as long as this murder lasted. John Roth had remained in that closet for twelve months, but the actual murder took only minutes to carry out." Tracy looked around the room. Fifteen sets of eyes were staring into his one. "It happened under everyone's nose; you just didn't know what you were looking at."

Tracy paused once more. He hoped Devin Thielberg was going to be impressed. "Starting this investigation, I felt at a disadvantage. I had no forensic evidence. No murder weapon. No eyewitnesses and no contents of the victim's stomach. Only a clothed skeletal corpse with a bloodstained floor beneath the body. I had to rely on the original report from the investigating officer and YOUR memories. So, I asked everyone the same question: *Who do you think committed the murder?* Many of your names were mentioned, some more than once. However, it turned out that no one provided me with the correct answer."

Tracy approached the Hollywood movie director. "Mr. Thielberg, you were perhaps the closest to the truth, even though you had just met most of these people, which made you the perfect unbiased observer. You told me that neither Miss Gabbard nor Miss VanHouten left the table during dinner. And then, screenwriter genius that you are, although you were guessing, you shared your perspective that it wasn't the wife and that the killer was a man." Tracy put away his notes and addressed the group with a sharp voice.

"I had little to work with when asked to take on this case. Two points stuck in my mind as I read the original report and examined the crime scene photos. The first was the photograph of Mr. Roth's Bentley and the image showing the placement of the front seat. As you recall, the car was discovered in the back lot of the country club the morning after his disappearance. While my predecessor focused on the vehicle's location, I noticed that the driver's seat had been pushed back to the last notch. When I reviewed the description of John Roth given by Mrs. Roth, she indicated her husband was short, approximately 5'6." This indicated to me that someone drove that car after Mr. Roth. Someone tall needed more legroom, so he moved the seat back. The second thing was the radio station placement."

Tracy put his hands in his pockets before turning to the assemblage. "And now let's begin the elimination of suspects with Mrs. Dora Crawley. Although your name never came up, I still considered you Mrs. C. But you had no motive and little opportunity." Tracy turned to the socialite. "So, if you will, please stand along the left wall with the staff members."

Dora Crawley glanced repeatedly at her husband but rose and proceeded to the wall.

"Even though your name came up as a possible suspect, I eliminated you, Mr. Winston. I was told that you went into the library that night. You were involved in a bad deal with Mr. Roth, which could have given you a reason to be angry with him, not to mention your height. But you were not the killer. So please join Mrs. Crawley and the staff." The handsome playboy stood and walked to the line forming against the wall.

"And next, I eliminated you, Mrs. Carrington. You had no motive and no opportunity to commit the murder. You can join the others." Christy Carrington did so hurriedly with a look of relief.

"Next, I considered our hostess, Mrs. Howell. Initially, I thought the motive was related to the note. However, after speaking with you today, I believe you were an innocent bystander who inadvertently disposed of our only evidence that a note ever existed." Tracy stepped over and offered his arm to the matronly lady of the mansion. He escorted her to the far wall where the others were gathered and then turned back to his guests.

"Next on my list of eliminations is Mr. Crawley. Even if you had a motive, such as this unfavorable business deal with John Roth, I couldn't find an opportunity where you could have committed this murder. So, I would say you are not the killer, sir." Richard Crawley didn't need to be asked to join the others. He leaped at the chance to leave his chair.

"And now, Mr. Carlisle, you may join the standing group. You meet the prerequisite of being over six feet, but you didn't kill John Roth, did you? Even though I'm sure you would have liked to on many occasions and for various reasons. And as much as I wanted it to be you, I love seeing Cagney as the villain; it didn't happen. You, sir, are not a killer."

Once Theodore Carlisle had left his seat, Tracy spread his arms out wide. "As you can see, ladies and gentlemen, there is a pattern here." Everyone stared. All the chairs on the left side of the room were empty.

James Howell

~~Dora Crawley~~	Bitsy Roth
~~Douglas Winston~~	Lawrence Winthorpe
~~Theodore Carlisle~~	Jacqueline VanHouten
~~Christy Carrington~~	Devin Thielberg
~~Richard Crawley~~	ZuZu Gabbard
Chair	Drake Carrington
(J.R empty seat)	

~~Constance~~ Howell

* * *

"It's curtains for them."
(Every gangster in every noir film ever made.)

Detective Tracy walked around the empty side of the table. He stood behind Mrs. Howell's empty chair. "As I said when I began tonight, this was a very tough case. Who had the motive and the opportunity to kill a man who was not present at the party? As Miss Penelope witnessed, a man came to this house and left in a taxi before any of you arrived, having let Mr. Roth out of the house herself. And there was the undisputed fact that his car was found the next day, still in the country club parking lot. I found the keys to the Bentley in Mr. Roth's blood-stained jacket pocket. So, did he return in the same taxi? Did he walk back here? Did someone give him a ride? Or was he killed somewhere else and put inside that closet at a later time?"

Tracy repositioned himself closer to the people standing along the left side of the table. "And, of course, the answer is that he never left. Mr. John Roth was here all along. While you enjoyed a wonderful dinner, Mr. Roth was inside that secret closet. I believe he was shown into the library by Reginald, left a note on Mr. Howell's desk, unlocked the French doors that led to the terrace while Reginald was out of the room, and then had the server, Miss Penelope, show him out. Once outside, he paid the taxi driver, let him go, and then snuck back into the library through the now-unlocked French doors. Mr. Roth only had a few minutes before Reginald returned to restock the bar."

It was Bitsy Roth who asked the question on all their minds. "So, what did he do, Detective? Did he spy on all of us? And why?"

"Because, Mrs. Roth, your husband may have wanted to hear for himself if you were in love with Mr. Carlisle, or he may have wanted to know if anyone was questioning his current land deal. The men would move to the library for cigars and bourbon at some point during the night."

Theodore Carlisle sputtered a rebuttal from the left side of the room. "Come on, Detective. You're fishing. Bitsy had nothing to do with J.R.'s murder. You have no evidence."

"I don't need evidence, Mr. Carlisle. And I haven't accused Mrs. Roth of anything."

"Good, and I'm sure you won't."

"But you can't deny the affair. Maybe Mr. Roth saw you coming out of the library together in the past. He knew if he weren't here at the party, the two of you would take the opportunity for a little rendezvous. I'm not asking if you met that night; I'm just telling you why Mr. Roth may have been there."

"What are you saying?" Bitsy demanded. "That I killed J.R.? You think you're clever in figuring out the affair. Is that why I'm still sitting here? Because I'm on your list of suspects?"

"You are about to be removed from that list, Mrs. Roth. You are guilty of infidelity, but not of murder. However, it is infidelity that may have led to your husband's death. You may now join the others against the wall."

Bitsy Roth shot Tracy an angry look as she rose to join the others standing. Theodore Carlisle wrapped an arm protectively around her shoulders as she slid between him and Christy Carrington. The six remaining seated exchanged silent glances: Devin Thielberg, Zuzu Gabbard, Drake Carrington, Lawrence Winthorpe, Jacqueline Vanhouten, and James Howell.

"I hope you're having a miserable time tonight, Detective. Because I know I am."

"I'm sorry, Miss Gabbard. I know this isn't easy. Just bear with me for a minute or two."

Tracy turned so his back was to the six. He addressed the dismissed people standing against the wall. "When I asked everyone who they thought the killer was, there was a unanimous show of hands on two points. The crime was either a crime of passion or a revenge killing for a wronged business deal. It's said that when you take away a man's pride AND his money, he'll do just about anything to get them back."

Jacqueline VanHouten jumped to her feet. She was still one of the ones sitting, and she didn't like it. "Look, Detective, I do not understand what you mean by passion. Am I still sitting here because I hinted that J.R. made a couple of advances toward me? Sorry, Bitsy, but that's the truth. Is that the reason? Ridiculous."

"No, Miss VanHouten. You are still sitting there because you were on the right side of the table that night. That's where the killer HAD to be. But remember, Mr. Thielberg provided your alibi. He said you never left the table. So, if it will make you feel any better, we can send you to the wall right now."

Jacqueline VanHouten threw back her head and crossed the room to the now crowded wall as Tracy turned back to the people still seated. He then began to walk around the room slowly. "I am confident that I know who committed this crime, and I can guess why. However, it is the mechanics of the crime that are so fascinating. When I spoke to each of you, and I admit I am as guilty as the rest of you, we all assumed that Mr. Roth was killed and placed in the hidden closet after the murder. But that is not how it happened. No. *John Roth put himself in that closet.*"

Lawrence Winthrope laughed out loud nervously. "The man had some good tricks up his sleeve, but...."

Tracy interrupted, "Mr. Winthorpe, John Roth went into that closet alive. He was murdered while he was in the closet. The killer went into the library, opened the hidden door, and stuck what I believe was a knife in Mr. Roth several times. The coroner stated that, given the angle Mr. Roth was sitting, a puncture at the base of the skull would have been fatal. By the way, Mr. Winthrope, you can join the others."

Lawrence Winthrope moved to his wheelchair and scooted across the room as Devin Thielberg, king of the Hollywood directors, raised a hand. "Why would the killer take such a risk, Detective? Mr. Roth might have cried out and fought back. And how did the killer know where J.R. was hiding if, as you claim, he put himself in there?"

"Either Mr. Roth confessed to suspecting that his wife was going to meet her lover in the library during the party, or he wanted to wait and hear what his investors were saying about the new land deal. He must have informed the killer that he would hide in the secret closet because he foolishly confided in him."

Everyone turned to the only man in the library with John Roth that night. Reginald shook his head as his feet suddenly started moving in time to a tap routine. "Detective. You have it all wrong. Mr. Roth didn't confide in me about anything. As I said, he left the note on the desk, and when I returned from the wine cellar, he was gone."

Tracy held up his hand, interrupting the butler's stream of objections. And the toe-ball-change. "I know you told me the truth, Reginald. You did not kill John Roth." Tracy turned back to the people still seated at the imaginary table. "But YOU did, didn't you, sir?"

* * *

"The one that everyone least suspected."

"He confided in you during drinks, didn't he? Mr. Carrington, you saw an opportunity, and you took it. You put a quantity of the migraine medicine in Mr. Roth's drink at the bar when he wasn't looking. The man probably told you himself that the drug took time to work. You knew he was only going six blocks and figured that by the time he got to the mansion and secured himself in the closet, the drugs would have started to work. Later that night, during dinner, you stabbed him. He didn't cry out because he was out cold. He may have even been dead already from an overdose, but you had to make sure. You took a chance that no one would return to this house for months. And you were right."

Christy Carrington stepped away from the wall. She was angry. And it showed. "What is this Detective? Are you accusing my husband of J.R.'s murder? Don't be ridiculous."

Tracy ignored the outburst and kept his voice calm and steady. "Mr. Carrington, I'm guessing you relocated Mr.

Roth's car. Assuming he wanted the Bentley to be less visible in the parking lot. He must have given you the keys and asked you to move it after he left. I also suspect that you took the Bentley for a little joy ride around the neighborhood since you had some time before you were expected at the party. You made three mistakes when you did. First, you moved the driver's seat to accommodate your longer legs. I'm guessing you are around 6'3." Second, you changed the station from the jazz channel, where Mr. Roth kept it, to the opera channel. By your wife's admission, you are an avid opera buff and the only man here who is. Thankfully, the original investigating Officer had the foresight to note the radio station when he started the car. And thirdly, you returned the keys to Mr. Roth's pants when you stabbed him, but you put them in the wrong pocket. You slipped them into his right pants pocket. Mrs. Roth told me her husband was left-handed. A lefty would have put them in his LEFT pants pocket. I should know."

Drake Carrington lashed out with a vengeance. "Detective, this is all just pure conjecture. My lawyer will tear your case apart bit by bit. What reason would I have to kill J.R.?"

"Debt, Mr. Carrington. Poor business decisions, insufficient funds to cover your gambling losses, and a wife who could spend quicker than you could earn. I discovered you owed John Roth for coming-due loans and didn't have the funds. I went to your bank and checked your account at the time of the murder. Aside from the debt, you're the only one who could have known Mr. Roth would be in that closet. Besides the staff, you were the last person to speak with him. It was clever. I'll give you that much."

"You have no proof. No murder weapon. No stomach contents after this length of time. You can't prove I gave J.R. anything. Like I said, my lawyers..."

"Oh, but I can prove it, Mr. Carrington. You see, Bitsy told me something that initially made me suspicious of you. She mentioned the migraine medicine. She was concerned about her husband taking too much of the medicine, so she counted the pills every day. The morning after the party, six were missing from the container. Enough to kill him or knock him out good. Since Mr. Roth accidentally left the medicine bottle on the bar when he exited the Country Club, the bartender kept it locked until he could turn it over. After the police returned the medicine container to Mrs. Roth, she told me she asked you if her husband had spilled some of the pills that day at the club, and you made the mistake of answering honestly."

Drake Carrington's color was beginning to fade from his face. "This whole thing is preposterous, Tracy. Exactly when did I commit this murder?"

"Mr. Carrington, you could only have one time, during dinner. All you needed to do was set yourself up. So, after you arrived and saw the table arrangement, you moved the place cards. Penelope said something was different. You were originally on the other side of the table but had to be near the library door, so you switched the place cards with your wife. It was the perfect setup. Mrs. Howell wouldn't notice you leaving as she is in her own world. And you knew that Miss Gabbard would keep Mr. Thielberg busy. So, at just the right moment, you slipped into the library. It didn't take long to stick the knife in a comatose man who was wedged into a closet. A powder room visit was your excuse if anyone caught you. But they didn't, did they? So, you returned to your seat without anyone noticing, or so you thought."

Tracy turned to Mrs. Constance Howell. "Mrs. Howell, I believe you provided key information I needed to clarify what happened in this room that night. You told me you saw Mr. Carrington get up from the table, leave the room, and return a minute later. There was no question in your mind."

Constance Howell stared at Tracy as if she were seeing him for the first time. Tracy had noticed from the first day that she showed signs of early dementia. Constance Howell experienced moments of complete clarity. Tracy had been present when one of those moments occurred. The remaining dinner party members looked at Drake Carrington with disbelief. Could it be true? Of course. Bitsy Roth sobbed quietly into Theodore Carlyle's shoulder.

"I'm arresting you, Drake Carrington, for the murder of Jonathan Roth. The officers here will read your rights and take you to the local precinct. You will have the opportunity to make a statement at that time."

Tracy concluded his interaction with Drake Carrington and then quietly exited the Great Hall as the officers escorted Mr. Carrington away. Behind Tracy, a group of people forever linked together and branded by the press as the Southampton 13, the socialites who witnessed the murder of one of their own. *The Fourteenth Man at Dinner, John Horatio Roth.*

Tracy was headed back to his home precinct (to the 19th). But this was not going to be "goodbye" forever. Oh no, not by a long shot...

NO BODY, NO HARM, NO FOUL

PROLOGUE

"Life is a game; money is how we keep $core"

New Yorkers are quick to point out that, "In the Hamptons, two scents linger heavily in the air (other than the smell of the sea, cold and salty), and those two ever-present scents are the fragrant bouquet of' old dusty money" and the savory spice of' newly minted" legal tender. The Problem: Old and new money are like oil and water; they don't mix well at any level, even though their lawns may touch, like intruding and uninvited guests at dinner.

"Old money" feels as if it has entitlement, having long been established by generations that have followed on the heels of our founding fathers and uncles. Old money has names on the bottom of the Declaration of Independence. It has roots and history, gathering dust for a purpose. Hand-me-down wealth is an assurance of immortality: a name on a building, a school grant, or a park, and the starting name on a string of names attached to an established law firm.

"New money" is the crisp upstart attempting to catch up with old money, even though it knows it never can, as old money has too much of a head start. New money is trying, sometimes pitifully, to bring itself alongside old money, but it's destined to be the "new kid in town" no matter how many zeros are in the bank account at J.P. Morgan. Therefore, it wasn't surprising to those who profess to be "old money" in this exclusive part of Long Island to learn that one of the "new money people" had gone missing. Of course, everyone was in a dither. No one wanted to see anyone harmed. Not since John Roth had disappeared in December of 1977 had there been such an uproar on both sides of the money tree. How could this happen? Who was responsible? Four days into the investigation, one of the detectives on the case suggested that they call in some help, as no answers were forthcoming. They asked what the name of that detective from the Manhattan 19th precinct who had assisted a few months ago on the John Roth case was. Then, someone came up with the answer.

So, on a beautiful morning in February 1979, one of New York City's finest was summoned to the end of Long Island and the Southampton community. Chief Patton agreed to give up his number one detective for the case. Patton didn't like it. But he agreed with their logic; they were much more likely to find out what happened to Margaret Hensley Blakely with the assistance of New York's number one homicide detective...Nick Tracy.

* * *

"When money talk$, $ometime$ it say$ 'good-bye.'"

Detective Nicholas Allen Tracy arrived at the South Hampton police station at approximately a quarter to nine on Wednesday morning. He intentionally dressed "casually." He wore his well-worn James Dean/Steve McQueen jacket and khakis. In time for the last few drops of coffee in the pot, a remnant of a pastry that may have resembled a cheese Danish, and half of a cinnamon raisin doughnut, he found the selection slim.

After a few crass remarks about his "city" jacket and a round of backslapping with the Hampton boys, Tracy was given the file on the missing woman: Margaret Hensley Blakely. It seemed that dear young Margaret was regarded as a "crossover" by the residents of this tight-lipped, tightfisted community on the edge of the vast stretch of land known as Long Island. Crossover suggests she grew up in the "old money" Hensley household, but when it came time to marry, rather than someone like "dear old Dad," she crossed over and married Reid Blakely, a member of the "new money" group, who made his fortune with a chain of appliance stores across all five boroughs. These stores were quite successful. He earned the title The Appliance King through his flamboyant commercials. His nickname didn't impress the old money blue bloods, who were horrified by his exuberant antics as he wore a crown and danced on their television screens, proclaiming himself as the "King of Appliance Land." They looked down their surgically altered noses at "all this nonsense." To further fuel their growing mistrust, he had accumulated his wealth too quickly in many people's eyes. Now, it seemed his holdings were rapidly multiplying and surpassing those of his father-in-law in terms of wealth.

It was scandalous.

Tracy glanced over the details in the case. The report had been prepared by Hampton Detective Ansel Jones, who made a call on Reid Blakely at his estate and taken a statement when the man's wife had gone missing. The facts that Ansel Jones had been able to gather were listed:

1. The night before Margaret Blakely went missing, she and her husband dined at a local restaurant with two other couples: Mr. and Mrs. Emerson Goldstein and

Mr. and Mrs. Jamison Potter. They returned home around 11 P.M. According to Mr. Blakely, nothing inside or outside the house had been disturbed. The alarm was still engaged.

2. The following day (Sunday), when Mr. Blakely awoke around 10 A.M., Margaret (known as Margot to family and friends) was not in the house. The alarm had been deactivated. After searching the house, Mr. Blakely discovered that his wife's Rolls Royce was missing from the garage. Everything inside and outside the house appeared undisturbed and normal.

3. Mr. Reid Blakely called a few friends and family. No one had seen or heard from Margaret. He then went for a drive through the neighboring areas. Blakely said his wife was not a jogger and had no habit of leaving the house before noon.

4. Mr. Blakely found the Rolls Royce in a grocery store parking lot while driving around and immediately called the police. Mr. Blakely made sure not to touch anything, fearing he might disturb fingerprints and other evidence.

5. Upon examination, the team found the Rolls Royce had a bullet hole in the cushion of the front seat, driver's side. Further examination uncovered the bullet lodged in the backseat cushion of the Rolls Royce. Mrs. Hensley's large Louis Vuitton purse was found on the backseat floor. Mr. Hensley confirmed that nothing seemed to be missing. Cash and credit cards were in the wallet.

6. Forensics stated the bullet was from a 38-caliber weapon. It was free of blood and/or flesh; therefore, it did not pass through human tissue. No weapon was found inside or near the car. A thorough search was conducted. (The victim's husband later admitted to

owning a 38 that he used recently at the range. The attendant at the nearby range confirmed).
7. The store clerks were questioned. Several of them knew Mrs. Blakely, but no one had seen her that morning. The store manager, Ralph Watkins, stated that when he arrived to open the doors of the small market, the Rolls Royce was parked in the far corner of the parking lot.
8. Margaret Hensley Blakely has no police record, not even a traffic ticket. She is not employed and has no children.
9. No one has heard or seen Margot Blakely since.
10. Statements were obtained from the last individuals who saw Margot. The two couples from the previous night's dinner, the Goldsteins and the Potters, all four people stated that the Blakelys seemed happy. There were no arguments or problems. Statements from other friends and family members are all consistent. There were no marital problems. There was no discord in the marriage.
11. Mrs. Blakely has no medical issues and is not under a doctor's care—no history of mental illness. Tracy reviewed the statements from the Goldsteins, the Potters, and the market manager, who was the first to see the Rolls-Royce. This was a straightforward case: The classic A.B.C's of detective work:
12. The husband/and/or family member killed Margaret Blakely and disposed of her body. Or...
13. The wife ran off with some person or persons unknown. Possibly a lover. Or...
14. The wife was kidnapped from the grocery store parking lot by someone who knew they could ask for a king's ransom from some wealthy people.

Since no ransom note had been found and no ransom call had been made, the likelihood of a kidnapping remained slim. However, it was too early to dismiss the possibility of one forthcoming. This left two options, neither of which appeared particularly mysterious. Nonetheless, the Hampton police encountered difficulties in narrowing down any leads. Why was that?

Perhaps no one wanted to investigate and potentially anger someone with that much money? Additionally, perhaps all the statements above explained why they had called in a NYC police detective to handle the situation: make the connection, obtain the search warrants, and bring out the handcuffs. And they were right. That's exactly what Nick Tracy was about to do. It was called his job.

*　*　*

"When large amount$ of money are in the card$, it's be$t to tru$t no one."

Tracy went straight to the local forensics department and asked to see the bullet found in the backseat of the Rolls Royce. It was wrapped in an evidence bag and labeled (Blakely case #3569909). Unfortunately, it was disappointingly negligible. It was simply another bullet fired into a non-moving object with minimal relevance to anything. However, someone had gone to great lengths to shoot that bullet through the front seat of the Rolls Royce, undoubtedly as a warning to someone. Who? The husband? The family? The police?

Tracy went to the precinct's back lot to examine the Rolls Royce. Two assistants were reviewing the carpeting, dashboard, steering wheel, panel, and upholstery, searching for anything Ansel Jones might have missed. When Tracy asked, the taller one replied that there was nothing to report. There was no blood, no prints— everything had been wiped clean.

"Detective, there's one thing: the dashboard panel, including the clock, is smashed and reads 7:47. I thought you'd want to know."

Tracy made another note in his book and then thanked the men. The time was likely insignificant. Or perhaps Mrs. Margot Blakely had smashed the clock to provide someone a clue: 7:47? If this was an abduction, the kidnappers might have broken the clock. But why go through the trouble? Or a very good lame duck to throw everyone off the track. But off the track of what? Tracy went over everything one more time.

There had to be more to this case than the disappearance of a Hampton blue-blood. What was he missing? It was time to call on someone who knew something. Someone who hadn't consumed nearly as much alcohol (the liquid amnesia) on the night of the disappearance. Yes, Tracy was determined to dig and dig until his shovel struck something solid.

* * *

"Money can't buy love, but it definitely Improve$ your bargaining po$ition."

For some reason, Tracy felt compelled to stand when Mr. Beau Hensley strolled into his Hampton mansion's front room as if stepping onto his yacht, docked at the marina. He was tall, tanned, and effortlessly suave, much like a movie star. To Tracy's discerning eye, Margaret Blakely's father resembled a blend of Laurence Olivier and David Niven, with a hint of Rex Harrison for good measure. A manservant had shown Tracy into the vast, slightly drafty room and gestured for him to sit on the wrap-around sofa, covered in a velvety fabric the color of exquisite emeralds.

Beau Hensley joined him but positioned himself at the opposite end of the massive sectional, crossing one linen trouser leg over the other. The man removed the stump of the pipe between his teeth and turned to Tracy with raised eyebrows. He held Tracy's card in his hand, which he now eyed with curiosity.

"What can I do for you, Detective Tracy?"

"It's about your daughter, Mr. Hensley."

"Of course. I didn't think you were here to talk about the stock market. So, what can I do to help, although I'm sure our Margot will be coming home very soon. This may just be one of her little stunts to get attention. I have seen them over the years, Detective. When her mother was alive, they used to plot together. But now that Margot is on her own..."

"So, you don't believe someone kidnapped Mrs. Blakely?" Tracy interrupted.

"No. There would have been some sort of communication from the kidnappers by now."

"Perhaps. But if it isn't a kidnapping, then who do you think is behind the disappearance?"

"Why, Margot herself, of course. As I mentioned, she is quite the little prankster. Sometimes, one never outgrows these things, Detective, even at the age of 30."

"What can you tell me, sir, about the marriage?"

"I would not have chosen Reid Blakely as a son-in-law. However, that decision was beyond my control. I stayed in the background and allowed my daughter to make her choice. There's nothing wrong with Reid; I am skeptical about how long his money will last. He's investing his earnings from appliance sales in trendy tech gadgets that may lose their appeal. Fade away, that's my take. And then my daughter will be stuck with an unhappy husband whose every word will feel like an attack."

Tracy stood and put his notebook back in his pocket. Beau Hensley didn't bother to stand. "I will keep you informed, sir. If anything comes up, I may need your assistance. I want to find your daughter as soon as possible. I don't know if there has been foul play. I don't know anything yet." Tracy left the room and proceeded to the front door. Beau Hensley, on the other hand, did not move a muscle.

* * *

"People $pend money to buy thing$ they don't need to impre$$ people they don't like."

Detective Tracy entered the Blakely backyard through a side gate. He had received no answer to his knock at the front door, and judging by the sounds from the backyard, he likely would have had better luck finding someone in the rear yard. And he was right. Tracy spotted Blakely among the crowd. He stood in his jeans and corduroy jacket, directing traffic, involving men with shovels and backhoes and others simply watching the men with shovels and backhoes. It was a bit of controlled chaos that Tracy assumed would lead to a newly renovated backyard in the shadow of the vast and stately Hampton mansion.

Tracy approached Mr. Reid Blakely, a tall man with a deep tan and a formidable demeanor. The detective extended his hand, offering one of his business cards. "Mr. Blakely, I'm Detective Tracy. I wonder if I could have a word with you about your wife. I…"

The man stared down at the card and then up at Tracy. He had dead eyes like a shark. "Sorry, Detective, I'm not Mr. Blakely. I'm John Aimsley, the job foreman. Reid is over there." John Aimsley pointed to the corner of the yard. A short, slightly heavyset man with a shock of dark red hair stood by the future site of a massive swimming pool. He looked down as if assessing the depth of the hole. His old clothes resembled Goodwill rather than something off the rack at Brooks Brothers. Of course, Tracy had forgotten about the "Appliance King" and his outrageous ads. He should have remembered Reid Blakely from his commercials; that face was always front and center in most ads. However, they seemed to hide the fact that the man was short and portly, concealed by the oversized cape and fur collar.

Carefully stepping over piles of dirt and rubble, Tracy approached the corner. Once again, he handed over his card. "Mr. Blakely, I'm Detective Nick Tracy. I'm working on your wife's missing person case. I want to speak with you." The short, stocky man indicated the large backhoe and a spot in the corner of the yard out of harm's way. When they were at a safe distance, Reid Blakely turned around, facing in Tracy's direction.

"What can I tell you, Detective, that I haven't told the other flatfoots who came around? I told them to get out there, find Margot, and stop wasting time hanging around here."

Tracy consulted his notes. He ignored the rantings. "Before Mrs. Blakely went missing, you had dinner with friends the night before. I've read the statements from the Potters and the Goldsteins, and it appears that the evening was pleasant and uneventful. Can you recall anything that seemed unusual... in your opinion?"

Reid Blakely smiled. Slightly. "Aside from the annoying photographer wandering around taking pictures of everyone and then displaying them at the front door, no. She was so condescending that she made you feel like you had to buy the damn photos on your way out as if the cost of a good steak, some potatoes, and a slab of cheesecake wasn't enough to spend at that place."

"Who was this photographer?"

"Some woman named Shirley Pechonis. She's Greek. She goes to each table and takes a photo of everyone; she tells you the picture will be available at the front desk. There's no obligation, of course. You can take the photo, and if you want more, you can order them and have them delivered to your house." Reid Blakely imitated the presumed high, squeaky voice of Shirley Pechonis: "... It will be such a lovely memento of your wonderful night. You are such a handsome group. This table is my favorite. Everyone is so good-looking." Blakely made a pinched face like a Pekinese.

"Of course, she said the same thing at every table. I heard her."

"Did you and Mrs. Blakely buy your photo? How about the Potters and the Goldsteins?"

"We bought ours. And I'm not sure about the others. I think Bretta and Emerson bought theirs. Not sure about Anna and Jamison."

Tracy made a few more notes in his book as he talked. "The name of the restaurant is The Pelican Bay. Is that correct?"

"Yes."

"And when you and Mrs. Blakely got home, I understand the alarm on the house was still on, and there were no signs of anything disturbed."

"Correct. I also mentioned the picture because I told the other two detectives I thought someone might have seen Margot's photo on that wall. That Greek woman hangs up the photos and places names beneath each image. Perhaps someone recognized our names and figured out who Margot was—the daughter of Beau Hensley. Beau has enemies; many would love to settle the score with him. Taking his daughter could be a good way to do that."

"But there's been no ransom note, no phone call."

"True. But the night is young, as they say."

Tracy closed his book and shook hands with Reid Blakely. The man's hands felt soft and fleshy. "Thank you, sir, for the information. I will follow up with you once I have something to report. Please keep my card in case you hear anything from your wife, or feel free to call the local precinct. I'm staying here at the local motel while working on the case, and I will keep you updated."

"Okay, Detective. I feel a lot more confident with you. I didn't like that Jones fella. He seemed incompetent. But I have a good feeling about you."

* * *

"Don't go broke trying to look rich." $$$

Tracy stopped in at the Pelican Bay Restaurant. It was a nice "joint," as Reid Blakely would say—a throwback from the olden days when you needed a password to get in. Or you knew someone who knew someone—sort of a speakeasy vibe. When Tracy arrived, the place was filled with hungry patrons lingering over afternoon martinis after the midday rush. No one here worked. They all "lunched" in designer outfits that fit perfectly. Tennis garb (mainly shorts with a sweater trimmed with navy stripes and tied around their shoulders) had been to the tailor before they appeared on the green-surfaced courts.

After briefly exploring the spacious restaurant, with its tall windows overlooking the water, Tracy searched for Shirley Pechonis. A few inquiries guided him in the right direction, and he found the photographer in the back room, collecting photographs from a large counter. He introduced himself and then explained his visit.

"Miss Pechonis, I'm looking into the disappearance of Margaret Blakely. I understand you took a photo of her the night before she vanished. Do you have a copy of that picture?"

The photographer looked a little flustered, but she answered straight away. "I do, Detective. Mrs. Goldstein, who was also at the table that night, hasn't picked up her copy yet. She didn't want it mailed, so she's coming by this afternoon." Shirley Pechonis reached over to a stack of manila envelopes and pulled one from the bottom. "Here you go...I will need this one back; Mrs. Goldstein might be disappointed if she couldn't take that home."

Tracy examined the photo. It depicted six people sitting at a set table in the corner of the room. He recognized Reid Blakely and Margaret Blakely since seeing her picture at the precinct. The other two couples appeared ordinary— at least, ordinary for very wealthy individuals. The diamonds on the lady's fingers were as rocks, and their dresses were couture. The men appeared wealthy, sporting gold Rolex watches. Even Reid Blakely dressed in his finest; there were no backyard grubbies tonight. Tracy returned the photo to the photographer. There didn't seem to be much he could glean from the shot. Unfortunately, they were seated at the corner table, and the rest of the diners were out of view. Everyone was smiling...happy. No sideways glances or furrowed brows. It had been a waste of time but a necessary one. Tracy thanked Shirley Pechonis and left The Pelican Bay. Before he could call it a day, he had a few more stops to make and spend his solitary night at the motel coffee shop.

* * *

*"Wanna' $ee how people really are?
Wait till money i$ involved."*

Bretta and Emerson Goldstein were not home when Tracy visited their residence. The maid informed him that neither would return until dinner time. Tracy thanked the young woman, asked her to pass along his card to the Goldsteins, and requested that they call him.

Next, he stopped by the Potters' house, just a few homes away from the Goldsteins. However, a few houses away in the Hamptons felt like a long trek, equivalent to three or four city blocks. The Potters' maid welcomed him into the sunroom, filled with wicker furniture and bright yellow cushions. He settled in comfortably, admiring the lovely greenery when the Potters breezed into the room, their smiles lighting up their faces like those of Ward and June

Cleaver. Tracy was soon to find that the analogy was more than merely physical.

Jamison and Anna Potter were the brightest and most cheerful people he had ever met. Their happiness was almost giddy. They answered his questions as if they existed solely to assist Tracy with his investigation. "So, you two don't remember any unpleasantness the night the six of you had dinner at Pelican Bay? What can you tell me about that night?"

Anna Potter was the first to speak, or rather, she was the first to gush. "Oh, Detective! There was no unpleasantness at all. It was a fantastic night, filled with laughter and great friends."

"And the Blakelys seemed their usual self?"

Next, it was Jamison Potter's turn to spew unadulterated sunshine. "They were, Detective. They are such a loving couple. We enjoy their company. Of course, Reid can be a bit of a handful, but that night before dear Margot went missing, everything was quite remarkable. We had a great time and..."

"Do either of you know where Margot Blakely might go if she, say, ran away?"

The two turned to one another and then turned back. Jamison Potter still had the floor. "We couldn't begin to guess. Margot is a bit headstrong, but she loves her husband. I mean, who doesn't love The Appliance King? Those commercials are so entertaining, aren't they? I don't think running away, as you called it, would ever..."

"Okay, Mr. and Mrs. Potter, thank you for the information. I was wondering if I could borrow your phone; my pager just went off."

After Jamison Potter led Tracy to the phone on his desk, he left him alone. Tracy dialed the precinct and spoke with Detective Jones. "Been trying to reach you, Tracy. Reid Blakely called. He received a ransom note. You had better get over there..."

* * *

"Rich people are ju$t poor people with money."

    Blakely paced back and forth in his decorated living room. At the same time, Tracy reviewed the ransom note for Margaret Blakely's return and scrutinized the photograph of Margaret duct-taped to a metal folding chair, her eyes wild with indignation and fear.

    "When did these come, Mr. Blakely?"

    "Just a few hours ago."

    "And this photograph shows your wife? Are you certain? It's a little fuzzy..."

    "That's Margot, Detective."

    "Do you recognize anything else? I realize the picture is dark, but maybe the surroundings?"

    "No. I don't recognize anything. Don't you think I've spent the last hour reviewing every inch of that picture with a magnifying glass? Nothing looks even remotely familiar."

    Tracy examined the note. The abductors demanded a million dollars to be delivered to the train station and placed inside the janitor's closet before midnight tonight, or Mrs. Blakely would be killed. The letters in the note were cut out from a magazine- clever yet overdone, reminiscent of every dime store novel. No imagination required. "Okay, Mr. Blakely. I'm assuming that you want to pay the ransom."

    "Yes. I want to get it over with."

    "Okay. When you have the million dollars together, please place it in a briefcase or satchel and call me at the local precinct. I will be here to escort you to the train station. And then I will place a guard on..."

    "Hold it right there, Detective. You read the note. No police. No undercover. No anybody. Or they will kill Margot. I'm not taking that kind of chance with my wife's safety. Just let them have the money, and I will get my wife back. I will go to the train station alone, and you will not send anyone to watch over me like a three-year-old toddler."

Tracy nodded in understanding but didn't like it. The note had used Mrs. Blakely's familiar name, Margot, instead of Margaret, indicating that they knew her—someone close, someone bold enough to attempt a kidnapping. Not good. "Okay, sir. Let me keep the picture. It seems coincidental that Shirley Pechonis also uses a polaroid in her work. I need to tie up a few ends. Call me when you make the drop. Then I'll return to the house to wait with you until your wife comes home. I hope you know what you're doing. I dislike giving in to extortion, but if you are adamant about this…"

"Adamant, yes. Thank you, Detective. And now, I must get to the bank..."

* * *

"Money is the $ixth $ense that make$ it po$$ible to enjoy the other five."

Tracy returned to The Pelican Bay. Once again, he asked for Shirley Pechonis, the photographer. He was informed that she was out buying supplies and would be back soon. So, he straddled the bar and had a beer while waiting. He even thought about having a second when Shirley came strolling in with her arms full of boxes. Tracy jumped off the barstool and gave her a hand. He followed her to the back room. When he deposited the boxes on the counter, and she removed her coat, Tracy began the reason for his return visit. "I wonder if you could take a look at this picture, Miss Pechonis. Since you're a photographer, perhaps you could share your insights about the photo. I'm assuming it was taken with a Polaroid."

Shirley Pechonis examined the image of Margot Blakely. Her eyes widened when she noticed Margot bound to a chair. She exhaled the breath she had been holding. "This picture is unsettling, Detective. I assume it's from some kidnappers somewhere."

"Yes. What do you think about the photo? Is it authentic? Polaroid?"

"Yes, to both. There is something very faint in the background."

"I noticed the same thing, but it's so faint and unreadable. Maybe it's just shadows; I don't know. Could you get this enlarged so I can see what it is?"

"I'll take it to my supplier, where I get the duplicate photos done and ask him. Horace owes me a few favors. I could ask him to blow it up and clarify whatever it is. I'll meet you back here if you can give me an hour..."

Tracy spent the next hour in Blakey's driveway waiting for his return from the million-dollar ransom drop. When he returned, the detective and the husband reviewed what had occurred at the train station janitor's closet. It had been uneventful; after they had exhausted the subject and there was still no word from Margaret, Tracy excused himself. He returned to The Pelican Bay restaurant to meet with Shirley Pechonis in her back-room studio.

"I'm sorry, Detective. Horace is out sick today, so I left the photo there. He should be in later. I spoke with him on the phone; he said he would notify me. He will have to take a photo of the Polaroid and then blow up the positive when he has a negative."

"Okay, Miss Pechonis. I will wait for your call." But Horace, the photo expert, didn't come in until the next day when his "head cold" cleared enough for him to gather himself and show up at work, which was too bad. It could have saved Detective Nick Tracy a whole lot of trouble.

* * *

*"The time to $ave money
is when you have $ome."*

Tracy let himself into the Blakely backyard. He knew he would find Reid Blakely there, along with his foreman and workers operating the backhoes and sod scrapers. He was correct. As Tracy approached from his left, he saw Reid wiping his brow with a dirty handkerchief.

"Detective. You're just in time. I was going inside to check the answering machine to see if there was any word from Margot or the kidnappers. As you can see, she's not here yet." Reid Blakely handed Tracy a glass of lemonade. Tracy nodded his thanks. "I've been thinking, Detective, I'm wondering now if this whole thing was nothing but extortion by someone who knew that Margot was worth a great deal of money to me. Maybe someone who knew Beau Hensley would never pay to get his daughter back. Sure, he puts up a good show, but trust me, his money is more important than his daughter."

"That's a very harsh statement, sir. He seemed genuinely concerned when I spoke with him. And believe me, I've seen many forms of grief and sincerity. I can usually spot the fakers. Mr. Hensley didn't strike me as a phony."

"Look, Detective, I've known the man for many years, and I had dealings with him before Margot and I married. And there are many people out there who don't like him or trust him. When the ransom note arrived, my first thought was that someone who didn't like Beau Hensley and his shady deals might have wanted to get even. They may have seen Margot's picture in The Pelican Bay the other night, with her name, and followed us home to find out where she lived. Being Beau Hensley's daughter may have been what got her abducted from that grocery store parking lot."

"Maybe, sir. But why would..."

"Or she ran away with someone. A lover, maybe. I'm a bit older than Margot. And not as pretty. She may have found a mug she liked looking at over her morning coffee more than this one. I know you'll ask if I've had any suspicions lately, and then I will tell you I had a few. I don't think we can rule out either theory. Someone who didn't like Beau Hensley. Or a lover who convinced her to run away with him and to bring along a million of MY money."

"Okay, sir. Thanks for the lemonade. I'm going back to the precinct to file an update. If I need anything further from you, I will call. In the meantime, please let me know when you hear from Mrs. Blakely." With that, Tracy left the Blakely house and went to a pay phone to call Shirley Pechonis. He caught her just as she was going out the door.

"Horace called. He has the blow-up and described it to me. I will pick it up now. I think you'd better come over as soon as you can. I have a feeling you're going to want to see this detective."

* * *

"The rich don't work for their money. They let their money work for them." $$$

Tracy got a court order to search Reid Blakely's backyard. It took a little bit of convincing. He found it hard to go after the wealthy, as they play by different rules than the rest of us, but he convinced the judge it was necessary for the investigation. He laid out the evidence piece by piece, and the judge finally relented. The order he issued was for a search of the Blakely property. In particular, the backyard. Tracy served Mr. Blakely with the order. Afterward, he appeared horrified, angry, and then furious. Tracy spoke over his ranting. "I need to see the hole being dug for the pool. I need to see the fittings for the gazebo, the greenhouse, and all the excavation for the new terrace. And any other diggings for flowers, shrubs, trees, etc. All of it, sir."

"I'm going to fight this detective. I'm calling a friend of mine who is a judge. You're like a loathsome bulldog that doesn't let go once it latches on. I understand. But you're barking up the wrong tree, shrub, bush, and flower."

"If that's the case, sir, then we've wasted our time, but in the meantime, so that you know, it's not going to be pretty. We are going to be digging wherever your men dug. But I have convinced the judge that it's necessary for this case."

"What case? You don't have a body. I've told you already. Margot may have been abducted by someone angry with that father of hers. Or maybe angry at me. Not everyone loves the Appliance King if their new dishwasher doesn't work. And then there's the possibility that she may have run off with some lover somewhere. Without a body, you have no case, no murder. I want the name of that judge you cajoled into giving you this order."

Tracy signaled for his men to enter the yard, then turned to Reid Blakely. "I'll provide the judge's name if you think it's necessary. If I'm wrong, sir, then I accept that. In the meantime, have your men cease their activities and allow my men to take over. Give them the remainder of the day off and tomorrow as well. We will need time."

Reid Blakely stomped off without another word of protest. He was angry but not stupid; he must have known the more he protested, the guiltier he appeared. For the next forty-eight hours, Tracy's men dug up every inch of Blakely's backyard, concentrating on the holes and areas the foreman, John Ainsley, and his crew had already excavated. If Reid had killed his wife and buried her body, what a perfect spot to choose- an area under excavation. There would be no suspicions with all the fresh mounds of dirt. But it was all for nothing. After two days, Tracy had nothing to show for their efforts other than dirty jeans and mounds of dirt. Tracy returned the yard to Reid Blakely with his tail between his legs. He didn't apologize or grovel, but he silently realized he was missing something BIG. It was time to change everything around and go on a different assumption.

* * *

It's ea$ier for a camel to pa$$ thru the eye of a needle, than for a rich man to enter the kingdom of God.
(Matthew 19:24)

"I'm about ready to throw in the towel, Chief. I can't find any evidence that Reid Blakely killed his wife." Tracy could hear the Chief shuffling through papers on the other end of the line.

"So, tell me what you've got. The condensed version."

"A ransom note and a photo with no fingerprints. It could be a hoax to get money. Maybe Margaret Blakely ran off with someone and needed some ready cash. A million goes a long way. She may have known that her husband would never agree to a divorce; I get the feeling he is afraid of his father-in-law. Beau Hensley is quite a formidable figure with rumors of his ties to the syndicate. Maybe someone was out for revenge against Hensley, or there's another possibility that someone was out for revenge against Reid Blakely."

"So, now that you've re-dug the man's backyard for nothing, what are your thoughts?"

"I currently believe someone is trying to frame Blakely. He appears guilty. Conveniently, his massive backyard was being excavated—the perfect opportunity to dispose of a body. Then, of course, there was the context of the ransom photo and the fact that Blakely seemed more focused on the placement of his petunias than searching for his kidnapped wife. That's not a legitimate reason to arrest the man. If the marriage was troubled, it could have been just as problematic for Margaret Blakely. Perhaps she wanted to escape."

"It sounds like you're leaning towards a case of extortion, Detective. We must consider the possibility that the wife orchestrated the abduction. She may have even chosen a location that would appear suspicious in the photo. As you've pointed out, this could be a case of a frame-up with the husband as the patsy. He's paid the money. The only thing left is to allow the local precinct to reassume their case. You've done all you could."

"Okay, Chief. I'll wrap up my report and have a sit down with the guys here." Tracy hung up the phone and finished his list with great disappointment. After saying goodbye to the detectives in the Long Island precinct, he signed out and made the trek to his car parked in the back lot.

On the way back to the city, Tracy's mind was racing. He reviewed every detail of the case. Every indicator pointed to the husband, which might be what was bothering him. There were too many signs. It was as if someone, perhaps the father-in-law, had set the whole thing up to make him look guilty. Alternatively, maybe he and his daughter were in this together. On the other hand, perhaps months from now, there would be some form of communication from Margaret Blakely expressing her regret for running away; she would realize she was wrong to stage the whole thing and would ask to return home to her cozy little mansion with the new backyard. If Margaret or her father went to all that trouble- creating the bullet hole in the front seat of the car, writing the note, taking a photo, and staging the whole scene to make Reid Blakely look guilty- the question was why? What did they stand to gain? There was always something to gain with murder. That realization struck Tracy like a bolt of lightning in a winter sky: the one possibility he had overlooked.

* * *
EPILOGUE

Rich man $, poor man $, beggar man... Detective.

Detective Tracy and his lovely mother were dining at their favorite restaurant and weren't alone. They were joined by loved ones, a family reunion. It was a noisy bunch, but no one seemed to mind. Shouting over other people was part of the experience in this big Italian and Irish family. After dinner, Tracy and his mom broke away from the crowd for some alone time. They found a quiet corner in the back of the room and slid into several chairs. As always, Patricia Tracy wanted to hear about the outcome of Tracy's latest case. His success. Or was this case different? Tracy brought his voice down to the room's tone as he began. "...and you know about the bullet through the front seat of the car. I told you that the husband, Reid Blakely, owned a 38 gun. And there was evidence that the firearm had been fired recently. But he explained it away with a story about shooting at the local firing range. And that checked out."

"Of course, he could have used the firing range before or after he put the bullet in the Rolls Royce," Patricia stated.

"You're right. But there was no way to prove it either way. Then there was the ransom note and the Polaroid shot of Margaret Blakely being duct taped to a chair. When I had the photographer, Shirley Pechonis, blow-up the picture, there was a faint sign in the background—a big red arrow with the word DISHWASHERS over the top. The shot was taken in one of Reid Blakely's warehouses. You know he's the Appliance King, with appliance stores and warehouses. So perhaps someone in Blakely's organization planned the kidnapping. I kept thinking about that perfect spot to hide a body that would be covered forever by a couple of tons of cement."

"But you said your men excavated the backyard and found nothing. No body was found."

"Yes. I knew I was justified in getting that order. Someone was making it seem like Blakely had his wife kidnapped and then murdered. There was too much evidence—the bullet hole in the Rolls Royce, the cheesy ransom note, and the staged photo. From my experience, it looked like a big, elaborate setup. And if it was a setup, who was behind it? Who had the money and the power to pull this off?"

"The father-in-law? You said he was beyond rich. And you mentioned there was no love lost between the two men. Maybe Beau Hensley arranged the whole thing because his daughter asked for help to escape from her husband. With a million dollars, she could start over somewhere. Or I'm thinking maybe she pulled off the whole thing with help from someone else. A friend? A lover? Maybe she sent the ransom letter and the photo and then didn't show up at home, making it appear that after he paid the ransom, she was killed anyway. Then she could disappear. There would be no body and now no case. Tell me, am I on the right track?"

"All good ideas. But it didn't happen that way."

Tracy's mother looked her son in the eye. "Are you saying...?"

"Yes. I'm saying the person who had the time and money to set everything up to make Reid Blakely look guilty was Reid Blakely. He ensured he was back in that "dug up" backyard whenever I came over, staring at holes. Mr. Reid wanted the police and me to suspect him so we would dig up the backyard."

"So, he killed her that night after the dinner at The Pelican Bay and then waited?"

"That is my thought. When I returned to the city, I called the Hampton precinct and shared that theory. They delayed before going back out to jackhammer the concrete for the pool. That's when they discovered Margaret Blakely.

The Appliance King must have hidden her somewhere in one of his freezers located in one of his thirty warehouses until he found a way to get me to dig up his yard. Once that was accomplished, he returned and placed her under the spot where the concrete for the pool was set to be poured."

Patricia Tracy smiled. "Let me say it…the best place to bury a body is *somewhere the police have already looked.*"

Tracy leaned over and kissed his mother's cheek. Then he sat back in his seat and sipped his beer. The sweat from the glass dripped onto his James Dean and Steve McQueen jacket, joining the other droplets that had accumulated over the years; what could be more perfect.

THE WORD OF THE WINDOW WASHER WITNESS

9:38 A.M.

NYPD Detective Nick Tracy arrived at the scene around 9:38 A.M. He was the only member present from the NYPD. Tracy entered the building, passed the bare-bones security, and went straight to the manager's office, where he found utter chaos. He shouldered his way to the back of the room, confident he would find someone in charge; he located a slightly flustered, middle-aged man who looked confused.

The nameplate on the end of his desk told Tracy everything he needed to know: Waldo Higgins, Building Manager— a name out of one of his favorite English murder mysteries. Mr. Higgins fit the prototype perfectly. He was short, with a slight build, a shock of reddish hair standing on end, and a pair of thick-rimmed glasses perched on the end of his nose like they had taken root there.

"Hello, Mr. Higgins, I'm Detective Tracy from the 19th. You called the precinct regarding a murder. Perhaps you could give me a few details. First, can we remove anyone from your office that doesn't directly affect the case?"

Henry Higgins spread his arms out in frustration. "Be my guest, Detective. I would be eternally grateful if you can get them out of here."

Tracy nodded and turned around to face the gathering mob. Everyone was talking at once. And no one was listening to anyone else. Tracy raised his voice a few octaves. "Attention everyone... I am Detective Tracy with NYPD, and I need this office for a formal investigation. Could you all leave quietly, except for anyone directly connected with the case, anyone who found the victim, witnessed anything relevant, or anyone with knowledge of the victim or the perpetrator. Do you all understand?"

There was a collective bobbing of heads. And then, slowly, everyone left Mr. Higgins's office in single file until there were only four people left in the room: Tracy, Mr. Higgins, a tall, gangly fellow in gray uniform pants and a shirt that said Empire State Glass Cleaning and a woman in a very business-like suit wearing three-inch spike heels and Susie McNamara glasses on a chain.

"...Okay, that's better. Why don't we all sit down and talk about what happened here? Maybe over in the corner on the couch and chairs."

When everyone was seated, Tracy began again. "Okay, where is the victim's body?" Three deer-in-headlights spoke simultaneously. Tracy silenced them by raising his hand. Then, he turned to Mr. Higgins. "Why don't you answer first, sir."

Higgins adams apple bobbed up and down as he swallowed hard. "Detective, there's no body. Mr. Riley Ackroyd, who is standing here, works for the company we hire to wash the building's windows. The team was on their last set of windows this morning; they started early. Mr. Riley saw a murder occur on the 17th floor. But by the time he came down, told security, who alerted me we all got up to that particular office, there was no body."

Tracy turned to Riley Ackroyd. "What did you see exactly, Mr. Ackroyd? And I need every detail, please."

Riley Ackroyd, a young man in his thirties with features that can only be described as ordinary. He nodded his head in understanding. He was short, stocky, and unremarkable, blending into the patterned wallpaper like a chameleon. "I was just finishing up one of the last windows on the 17th floor; it was about 8:20 A.M. Johnny and Gus were around the corner. That's when I noticed a reflection in one of the mirrors. A man had another man in a stranglehold. He was choking him to death. The poor man's face was turning all shades...first red, then blue until finally the man doing the choking dropped the dead man to the floor. That's when he looked up and saw me watching him in the mirror."

"Did the man run away?"

"No, that was the funny thing. He calmly walked over to the window, smiled, then looked down the street seventeen floors below and started laughing. I believe I remember him heading to the door. Before he did, he paused at the desk, scribbled something on paper, tore off the sheet, and took it with him. When he got to the door, he turned back to me and started laughing again, like he knew it would take me a long time to get the scaffolding down to the street and then go in and call the police. He was mocking me big time."

"What did the man look like, Mr. Ackroyd? Old, young, tall, thin...?"

"He was average height, average build, but he had a close-cropped beard, glasses, and long hair pulled back into one of those ponytail things the guys wear nowadays. Oh, and he was wearing tan pants with a brown plaid jacket and a bright red necktie."

"How about the man he was choking? Can you describe him?"

"Not much to describe. He was wearing a business suit and a yellow tie."

"Facial hair?"

"No. From what I could see, he was clean-shaven and had short dark hair. That's all I remember."

"One more thing. The man doing the choking, you said you saw him in the mirror writing a note. Did he use his left hand or his right hand?"

"Left. I remember that distinctly."

Tracy noted the descriptions in his notebook, including Ackroyd's full name, address, telephone number, and the name of the window-washing company. He then snapped his book shut. "Okay, let's go take a look at the scene of the crime, Mr. Ackroyd. Mr. Higgins you can fill me in on the particulars, like who occupies the office."

The woman at the end of the couch stood abruptly. "That would be me, Detective. I'm Judy Hernandez. I'm the present occupant of office number 1712."

Miss Hernandez had an interesting face. Not pretty, just interesting. Like a co-star in a major motion picture where all the leads are wildly attractive. (Olivia DeHaviland as Melanie, second fiddle to Scarlett, who of course stole the show). Miss Hernandez said she rented the space from the company occupying the seventeenth floor, a big financial firm. Ms. H was dating one of the financial advisors at the firm. He recommended her for the space when it became available. "How long have you been there, Ms. Hernandez?"

"Oh, about six months, Detective, and before you ask, no, I don't know anyone who fits the description the window washer gave. When I got here at nine this morning, I was escorted into Mr. Higgins's office by building security, and I haven't been up to see if anything is missing in my office. I'm sure that was your next question."

Tracy smiled slightly. Everyone was always trying to beat the police to the punch. "Ms. Hernandez, thank you. I'm afraid you can't go into your office until we have collected evidence and dusted it for prints. So please wait here."

With that, the three men filed out of Mr. Higgins' office and down the long corridor to Security. Tracy showed his badge and requested that his party be escorted to office #1712. Before leaving the security office, Tracy called for his forensic team to come and collect any evidence. He then joined the group in the main elevator. Everyone remained silent on the ride up to the 17th floor. Higgins coughed once, but it was more of a nervous tic. When they reached office 1712, Tracy told everyone to hold back. They complied, but it really wasn't necessary. When the security man guarding the door stepped aside and opened it, there was nothing to see. No body, no blood, no person of interest. Nothing appeared disturbed. It was a nice, tidy office, except for the half-cleaned window overlooking Lexington Avenue.

* * *

10:17 A.M.

Four individuals—Tracy, Riley Ackroyd, office manager Higgins, a security guard named Sam—began their search for a killer and a dead body on the seventeenth floor. They checked each office, storage closet, bathroom, lounge area, company kitchen, and conference room. Riley Ackroyd was instructed to observe every individual at each desk. Through the process of elimination, the seventeenth floor was cleared. No faces appeared familiar to the window washer. They moved on to the sixteenth floor, repeating the same routine. It seemed they were getting nowhere fast until they dropped their search to the eighth floor. In the main hallway, they encountered a young man pushing a trash cart. He was part of the building maintenance team.

Mr. Higgins made the introduction. "This is Mike Evans, Detective. He collects the morning trash from each of the floors. Usually, there are no more than paper coffee cups and breakfast wrappers. The early afternoon collection yields more results. We like to keep a neat building."

Tracy looked inside the trash bin on wheels. There was very little in the way of garbage. "So, Mike, is this your first round this morning?"

"Yes Detective. But my second bin. Earlier, I had to go to the dumpster. My bin was too heavy, and I..."

"Wait...Heavy? Where is this dumpster? Take me to the dumpster...now." Tracy had Mike, the trash collector, place his bin against the wall and lead the way to the nearby service elevator. Mr. Higgins and Riley stayed behind. Tracy silently rode to the basement. When the elevator doors opened, Mike pointed to the dumpster he had used earlier. Tracy whistled a nearby maintenance man and had him grab a flashlight. Together, the three men searched through the bin. Nothing. No dead body. Nothing. The maintenance man, Jack, mentioned he saw someone rummaging through the dumpster earlier. The man claimed he had accidentally discarded something. He didn't fit the description of the suspect. It was another dead end with no body.

* * *

11:03 A.M.

When Tracy and Mike, the trash boy, returned to the eighth floor, Riley Ackroyd and Mr. Higgins had completed their eyewitness search. Nothing turned up—no familiar faces. When Tracy caught up with Ackroyd, he was talking to a woman in a tight-fitting dress with an entire tube of lipstick smeared across her lips. She spoke rapidly, gesturing with her hands like some of Tracy's Italian relatives. As Tracy approached, she immediately turned her attention to him.

"You must be the Detective I'm hearing about. I'm Alice Johnson, in sales. I was telling Mr. Ackroyd here that

I saw a man earlier who fit the description of the man he saw in the window. I'm sure it's the man you're looking for."

"Where did you see the man, Ms. Johnson?"

"In the hallway, right outside the main elevator. He was munching on a toothpick and talking to himself. I may have seen him before here in the building. Not sure. But today, I remembered the beard, the long hair, the glasses, and the red tie. He looked suspicious. I said, 'Alice, that guy is up to no good. I wonder how he got by Bernard in security?' Then, when I turned around, he was gone."

"And you say it was on the main floor?"

"Yes."

"What time?"

"Around 8:30 or 8:45 A.M, maybe. I can't be sure. I came in early to catch up on some paperwork. I wasn't paying much attention to the time, Detective."

"And you didn't see the man again, Ms. Johnson?"

"No. Not again."

"Okay, thank you. You can go. But here's my card, just in case you happen to come across him somewhere here in the building. If you do, I would appreciate a call."

Alice Johnson nodded once and then went on her way. All three men watched after the tight-fitting dress and then turned back to one another. Tracy spoke first. "Mr. Ackroyd, please do me a favor and don't speak to any witnesses. The worst thing witnesses can do is talk to one another. Then the story in your head gets updated."

"Okay. I get it, Detective. I wasn't listening much to Ms. Johnson. It was more like I was staring and wondering to myself how anyone could get that much makeup on their face."

* * *

11:28 A.M.

By the time the group of four men reached the fourth floor, they found themselves in a hub of activity: people milling around and talking. The search for the body was the main topic within the building. Tracy, the window washer, the building manager, and the guard navigated through the crowd. Who knew there were so many people with nothing to do on a Tuesday morning except to follow the search for a body? From the snippets of conversation, it seemed that everyone had a sighting. Everyone on the fourth floor had eyes in the front and back of their heads; they had seen everything and everyone. Tracy stood on a chair, needing to rise above the crowd.

"Excuse me, everyone. My name is Nick Tracy, and I'm with the New York Police Department. As you all know, I am looking for a body and a possible killer to go along with it. If you have information regarding this case, please stay where you are. All of those with no concrete information and no eyewitness report, please leave the area and go back to your offices. Thank you for being so cooperative."

A buzz of disgruntled voices arose from those shuffling slowly away from the area. When the crowd cleared, two people, a man and a woman, stood watching the dispersal. Tracy turned to the woman first as he stepped down from the chair. "Okay, Ma'am, let's start with you. What's your name, and what did you see?"

The short, stocky woman wearing a flowered dress spoke up timidly. After stating that her name was Mary Wu, she launched into a brief narrative. "Well, I'm not sure how significant it is, Detective, but I saw a man who matches the general description. He's in one of the offices behind me on the fourth floor. I inquired about him, and someone told me he was a paralegal on loan from another law office. He doesn't appear suspicious or anything."

"What does suspicious look like, Ms. Wu?"

Mary Wu blushed a few shades of crimson. "Oh, you know, Detective. Sort of out of place, slippery, eyes always darting around the room, that sort of thing."

"Okay, go on. What was he doing that made you suspect him?"

"He matched the description I had heard around the water cooler. And he is new to the building. He was tapping his foot as if he were nervous or something. Does that make sense, Detective?"

"Well, those are all reasons to suspect him, I understand, but you didn't happen to notice if he had a dead body with him."

Mary Wu let out a hearty chuckle. She was a good-natured soul. "Don't be silly, Detective. I know you're having a bit of fun at my expense, and I understand that a touch of levity is beneficial when discussing a serious subject. I would appreciate it if you wouldn't dismiss my observations as frivolous. I am quite intelligent."

Tracy suddenly felt bad he had made a comment questioning her better judgment. "I'm sorry, Ms. Wu. You're right. Now, can you tell me where this man is?"

Mary Wu nodded and started down the hallway with the four men trailing. When she arrived at Pennington, Krause, and Goldstein, she pointed to a thirty-something young man pecking away on a typewriter in the near corner of the office. He had a close-cropped beard, hair pulled back into a ponytail, and wire-rimmed glasses. He was tapping his foot, just as Mary Wu had mentioned.

Tracy watched for a moment. The young man didn't look up; he didn't hardly move a muscle. He just kept his head down and continued to type. There was a glass of water sitting to the right of his typewriter. Tracy wanted to see the man pick up the glass and take a drink, which he did a few moments later. Tracy nodded just as he thought. Righthanded. He turned to Riley Ackroyd. "Does that man back there in the corner look familiar Mr. Ackroyd?"

Riley Ackroyd strained to see, but he shook his head in the negative once he had focused. "Afraid not, Detective."

Tracy turned to Mary Wu. He wanted to make up for the insensitive remark earlier. "Ms. Wu, thank you for your observation. It has been helpful. Here's my card if you notice anything or anyone else who appears suspicious."

After Mary Wu left the area, Tracy gathered the other three men and returned to the foyer. The lone man was still there, standing in the middle of the room. His look seemed to say, "I have something important you need to know..."

* * *

12:14 P.M.

The man extended his right hand to Tracy. "Hello, Detective Tracy. My name is Gavin Moore. I work here on the fourth floor."

"What did you see, Mr. Moore?"

"I arrived early—earlier than usual. Went to the men's room, likely due to too much coffee, if you catch my drift. When I walked in, a man was washing his face. It's not something you see every day."

"What did the man look like?"

"Oh, I would say he was a big man, husky. He had thick hair, brown."

"Was he clean-shaven? Or did he have a beard?"

"No, he was clean-shaven alright. Very clean."

"What about glasses?"

"Nope. No glasses."

"What was he wearing?"

"A black short-waisted jacket and tan pants."

"Did he speak to you?"

"No. We just nodded in passing. I went into one of the stalls, and when I got out, he was gone."

"Mr. Moore. Here's my card. If you see the man again or remember anything, please let me know. I appreciate your feedback."

Mr. Moore took Tracy's card and turned back to him with a glimmer in his eye saying… "Detective, a few months ago, I noticed something in the restaurant's first-floor kitchen. This ancient building has been updated to modern standards, yet a few old features remain. In one corner, I saw they hadn't removed the old dumbwaiter during the remodeling; it's still there. I thought you might like to know. That would be the perfect way to transport a body up or down. I'm just saying."

Tracy's mind started to race a bit. Mr. Moore may have been right about that…

* * *

12:48 P.M.

The search for the dead man and the killer continued. Tracy made a note in his book to check on the dumb waiter (a food transporter), and they proceeded down to the third floor. At one point, Mr. Ackroyd thought he saw a man who fit the description of his perp. But it was a false alarm. The man was one of the security guards who was home having breakfast at the time of the incident.

Tracy was starting to get a bit frustrated with the progress, or lack of it. And that's when he met a woman named Mary Ann Jacobs boarding the elevator behind his party of four as they proceeded down to the second floor. Where there's a will, there's a witness. Mary Ann Jacobs was the epitome of the phrase "secretary." Tracy would never have expressed that observation aloud; his women's libber friends would have taken him to task for it, but it was true. She wore a two-piece business suit that fit her perfectly. She had a pair of pink glasses perched on her well-scrubbed, makeup-free face, with a barrette in her mousy brown hair, cut close to her head at a length that his other hairdresser friends would call a "bob." She was attractive, yet not in a way that would evoke jealousy in a wife if her husband worked late. Mary Ann was perfect, intelligent, articulate, and invaluable. As she entered the elevator, she turned to Tracy as if they had been introduced and were working closely together.

"My name is Mary Ann. You might want to make a note of that Detective. I came from the restaurant a few minutes ago. I had an early lunch. And as I was leaving, I noticed this man supporting another drunk man. Normally, I would never have paid attention, but it was the middle of the day. Who drinks so many cocktails at lunch that they end up stumbling drunk and need to be helped out of the bar? How do you return to your desk, or even your office, in such a condition?"

Tracy stared at Mary Ann Jacobs. It was a moment before he answered. "Do you remember what the man looked like, Ms. Jacobs? The one who was doing the supporting?"

"Yes. I do. He was a rather ordinary man, and if you are going to ask me to describe him facially, I would say he was clean-shaven, with short, cropped, thick hair pulled back away from his face. He had brown eyes and teeth a bit crooked; he never got braces as a kid, is my guess."

"What about his clothing?"

"Black...what women call a blouson type jacket... tan pants and a white shirt beneath the jacket."

Where had Tracy heard that description before? Maybe it was Gavin Moore. Tracy turned back. "Would you say, Ms. Jacobs, that the man had a very clean face and hands?"

"Well, now that you mention it, Detective..."

***

1:09 P.M.

Tracy sat in office #1217 belonging to Judy Hernandez on the seventeenth floor of a high-rise building in midtown Manhattan. He stared out the window at the spot where Riley Ackroyd had dangled high above Lexington Avenue when he spotted a murder reflected in a mirror. Then, he made a list of everything he knew about the case. It was all about the perp; he knew nothing about the victim.

Window Washer Witness Case - January 1979
1. The murderer wrote something on a piece of paper before he left this office.
2. The murderer was left-handed.
3. The murderer had a ponytail, glasses, a beard, plaid jacket, tan pants, and a red tie.
4. The murderer had more than enough time to get away, but did he?
5. The murderer couldn't just walk out carrying a body over his shoulder.

Tracy stopped writing, putting the pen down as he went in search of Mike Evans, the trash collector. He found him pushing a bin on the ninth floor during the afternoon run.

"Detective Tracy, what's up?"

"Mike, I was wondering if, by chance, there were any other dumpsters for the building. We only searched the east side. Are there dumpsters on the west side also?"

"Yes, sir. I only took you down the east side because the west side service elevator was out of order. When I went to take down the morning bins, a sign said, 'out of order.' I believe the sign is still there. It's the side the restaurant kitchen uses for garbage and such."

Tracy grabbed Mike Evans by the arm and pulled him forward. "Okay, Mike, let's find that elevator and the west side dumpsters. Not until after we check out the dumb waiter in the kitchen."

With that, the two set off toward the kitchen. The central kitchen for the building's restaurant was located on the first floor. It buzzed with activity as chefs, assistants, waiters, and busboys vied for space. Each appeared to shout over the other, creating an almost comical scene. Tracy and Mike found the old contraption in the corner of what was now an enormous pantry. When they pulled up the chute, there in plain sight was the dumb waiter itself. It was obvious there had been three inches of dust...until recently. A smear of clean surface was evident across the length of the 36" square lift. Someone or something had been a guest of the antiquated features of the old building in the last few hours, and Tracy had a pretty good idea of who it was.

* * *

1:26 P.M.

The ride down to the basement was a short one. Mike Evans filled Tracy in on the locations of the west side dumpsters. He said they were hard to miss. He was right. Tracy and Mike spent over an hour going through the west side trash holders. They were large, and they were smelly. But it had to be done. Unfortunately, their efforts revealed absolutely nothing in the way of answers as to where the body went. When they backed away from the huge walk-in containers, the men smelled almost as bad as the trash. Tracy was beginning to doubt the window washer's story.

But what possible motivation could he have for seeking attention? Or could that be the answer? And where was the "dead man?" No one had reported anyone missing from the building. Mr. Higgins had circulated descriptions of both men to all floors, and so far, nothing. If the dead man didn't work in the building, that would be another story. They would have to wait for a missing person report.

Tracy had called his office and asked for a hurry-up on the fingerprint I.D. Ms. Hernandez had provided hers, so it was just a process of elimination. Ms. Hernandez said she didn't get visitors, and no one else had been in the office since it had been cleaned two days ago. So, any prints might belong to the perp or the dead man. As Tracy and Mike Evans returned to the service elevator, Tracy noticed several doors that led somewhere. He asked Mike Evans.

"These are storage lockers, cleaning supply rooms, maintenance equipment, and a few units that the building rents to individuals wanting to store items."

Tracy nodded silently but his wheels were spinning. It could be a great place to hide a dead body. He told Mike Evans to go up to Mr. Higgins office and let him know that Tracy wanted to see inside the storage units. Then, get the master key to all of the units from the maintenance staff and meet him down here in 10 minutes. He then radioed a code 10-2 for backup.

Less than five minutes later, two patrolmen whom Tracy knew well appeared at the front desk asking for him. He came down the elevator and approached the two familiar faces. "Well, Ramsey and Jackson...of all the gin joints..."

"Hello, Detective Tracy. What can we do to help? We have our orders to stay with you."

Tracy gave Ramsey and Jackson the master key, directed the officers to the basement and told them to open each and every door while he went back upstairs to question Riley Ackroyd further. This could be the break he needed, or it could be a dead end. Either way, it was worth the effort. Perhaps his earlier thoughts were correct: Riley Ackroyd was either a nut or a psycho- or worse. Maybe the window washer saw his reflection in that mirror.

* * *

2:31 P.M.

"I'm telling you the truth, Detective. Honest. I saw what I saw. I have given you every detail."

"Let's go over this again, Mr. Ackroyd. You saw a man strangling another man using a chokehold. You have described him; I got that. But there must be something we are missing. You said he came over to the window, looked you right in the eye, and laughed."

"Yes. He was taunting me, almost daring me to come after him. He didn't try to hide his face or anything. He knew how long it would take me to get down and run inside to call the authorities. He had plenty of time. Only a handful of people were in the building that early in the morning. And none on the seventeenth floor. I know. I asked the other window washers who were around the corner from me. We could see inside the offices. They were empty. There were no people, no lights on. Except #1712."

"You see, that's just it, Mr. Ackroyd. How did he manage to get the body out of the building? He might have used the service elevator to transport the man to a lower floor, possibly even to the kitchen. The dumb waiter would have worked. And later even came right through the restaurant door, dragging the man like someone who might have had too many martinis. But where did he go from there? Where did he put the body? Mr. Higgins and I checked all ten of the camera footage from outside the building. No one left this building after you came down from that scaffolding. Not a person, not a vehicle, not the garbage men, no one. And no one left carrying a body. So how is that possible?"

Patrolmen Joe Ramsey and Brande Jackson had completed the inspection of the basement. They waited in the hallway for Detective Tracy to leave Mr. Higgins's office. When he emerged, Jackson spoke for both of them. "Sorry, Detective. I wish I had better news. We checked that basement thoroughly; I mean, we checked every door and every cubbyhole. We didn't find anything- no body."

Tracy nodded. He knew if there had been anything to find, these two would have stumbled upon it. "Okay Jackson, thanks. Did you cover the back wall doors and exits and… look, why don't we just go down together, and you can show me."

3:00 P.M.

The three NYPD members arrived in the basement on the west side. Officers Jackson and Ramsey showed Detective Tracy where they had been and checked every door they had opened, along with every dark corner they had investigated. They had nearly completed their rounds when Tracy noticed a large double door at the end of a wide corridor.

"How about this hallway here? This isn't a maintenance storage room, is it?"

Again, Jackson answered for the two. "Naw. Just a walkway to that artist's studio."

"What artist?"

"The guy using that warehouse space for his studio mentioned that he rents it from Higgins. We spoke to him briefly. He's friendly and noted he hasn't seen or heard anyone prowling around the basement."

"Wait a minute. I didn't see any artist studio on Higgins building plans."

"We would have missed it too if it hadn't been for this long corridor. We followed it and checked it out just to be sure. There he was. I think his name is Gino. An Italian guy. If Higgins didn't mention him and he's not on the building plans, that sly fox is probably pocketing the rent money each month."

"Yeah. Maybe. What kind of art? Like Andy Warhol-type stuff?

"No, nativity scenes for the Christmas season."

Tracy thought for a minute. "Okay, let's go guys. Perhaps this artist knows more than he realizes. If he had taken the service elevator on the east side, he might have seen something significant without knowing it. Let's assess what this Gino knows."

Tracy didn't need to repeat himself. Ramsey and Jackson followed in his footsteps until they reached the end of the corridor. Tracy threw open the door. Mr. Gino Rispoli was in all his splendor. He was dressed in a bright orange painter's smock over an electric blue jumpsuit, wearing a jaunty red beret tilted on his head, dipping down over one eye. Mr. Rispoli was up on a ladder, completing his latest creation: a wise man wearing a long, flowing garment and following the brightest star to Bethlehem.

Rispoli descended the ladder and extended his hand to Tracy. The man had forearms like a longshoreman and a face like Marcello Mastroianni. When Tracy explained who he was, the artist smiled and offered an invitation in his broken English. "Please... feel free to look Detective. Let me know if I can assist."

Tracy shook the man's hand again and walked over to one of the dozens of nativity scenes scattered through the area while Jackson and Ramsey looked behind closed doors. After a few passes down the aisles containing rows and rows of plaster figures, wise men in one spot, three kings and baby Jesus with his parents in another, Tracy signaled for officers Jackson and Ramsey, who welcomed the sign to meet outside, as this Gino Rispoli was a talker of major proportion. He possessed boundless words to correspond with his limitless supply of paint cans.

Outside in the parking garage, the three men compared notes. It appeared the window washer had been mistaken about witnessing a murder. Perhaps the "strangler" had choked a man just enough for him to lose consciousness. Maybe he woke up shortly after the bearded man with the ponytail and red tie left the office and went home feeling unwell. Jackson offered a suggestion. "You know what they say, Detective. You can't win 'em all."

Detective Tracy smiled. "You know who said that, Jackson?... a loser."

* * *

3:37 P.M.

The parking garage was still full. It wasn't quitting time yet, and the building buzzed with daytime workers. Those working in the building could enter, park their vehicles, and go to their offices. However, no vehicles were able to depart. Tracy looked around at all of the cars. That's when it occurred to him: the killer could have placed the body in the trunk of one of the cars parked here. So, he went back to Mr. Higgins office and ordered a copy of the CCTV tape of the parking garage. He wanted to see how many cars were parked when the murder occurred. Since all the vehicles were still there, he only needed to search for those cars. The surveillance tape was put on the monitor, and Higgins and Tracy were looking at it.

There was a total of eight cars on the tape. Tracy made a list of every vehicle and occupied parking space number. He then went to find Ramsey and Jackson. He had the two patrolmen locate every owner of the eight vehicles. Each of the trunks was opened. Each car was searched. Nothing. There wasn't a dead body anywhere in any trunk. As far as Tracy could see, this building had no dead body. Which meant there wasn't a killer here either.

Tracy was just thinking that Jackson may have been right. There was no way to win here, just lose more slowly, when he decided to go back upstairs and chat with Mr. Higgins before giving the go-ahead for people to leave the building. For added security, every car was searched before it left the parking lot. The killer may have somehow placed the body in an unlocked vehicle that drove into the garage. Tracy remembered one of his original witnesses, Alice Johnson, and something she had mentioned. He consulted his notes. The possibility that the murderer might not have needed to get past Bernard, the security guard at the front desk, made sense if the murderer worked in the building. Walking quickly through the basement, Tracy ran into the artist, who returned from getting a coffee from across the street. He waved Tracy over and asked him a few questions about the investigation as they continued walking toward the artist's studio, and Tracy followed him inside.

He admired the man and his nativity work. When the artist went to put on his apron, Tracy pushed one of the figures aside- it was the figure that Rispoli had been working on earlier, one of the wise men. He then turned and watched as Rispoli pushed a figure aside to make room for Joseph, then Mary, one of the three Kings.

"Detective, would you like to see some of my sketches? In the back?" Tracy nodded "yes" and followed the artist. When Rispoli opened the door to his little hidden gem of a work studio, that's when it hit him. Like the first wise men following the brightest star to Bethlehem, he suddenly knew what he had almost missed. The search of the garage, the search of the offices, the search of the closets, cubbyholes, supply rooms, and maintenance all led up to this. The moment the best detective in the NYPD force realized precisely what the killer wanted him to know and not know.

* * *

8:45 P.M.

The Chelsea Café, midtown Manhattan

"Detective, you've kept me in suspense long enough. What happened? And this had better be good."

Tracy took another sip of his beer. It tasted good. Maybe it was a little bit too much fun torturing his favorite cousin. He relented.

"Okay. It's like this...we knew the killer was a man with a ponytail, a beard, and glasses wearing a plaid jacket, tan pants, and a red tie. We had the description from the very beginning from the eyewitness, the window washer Riley Ackroyd. Through deductive reasoning, we soon figured out that the killer moved the body from the 17th floor via the trash bin. It was handy because Mike Evans always started his morning trash collection on the top floor of the building and worked his way down to the basement, so he stored the push bin up on the top level. And the killer knew this. So, he used the nice handy bin to transport the body. And the window washer said that before the killer left Ms. Hernandez's office, he wrote something. It was an 'Out of Order' sign to put on the west side service elevator so no one would use it. The killer then went into the restroom and removed his wig, his fake beard, his glasses, and his red tie, which, was on purpose; in case someone saw him, he wanted to send the lookers in the direction of a man with that description. Next, he turned his plaid jacket inside out, revealing a black lining. Before leaving the bathroom, he washed the beard glue off his face. That's what Mr. Moore saw when he entered that men's room. And then he moved the body down to the basement..."

"What about the dumb waiter you mentioned earlier?"

"Yeah, about that...I thought I had something there, but it was nothing. One of the busboys in the kitchen was playing a joke on the chef the other day, and he hid in the dumb waiter."

Cousin Tony laughed out loud. "What about the guy carrying the drunk out of the bar?"

"False alarm. Some guy was drowning his sorrows over a liquid lunch, and his buddy gave him a hand back to his office to sleep it off."

"Okay, Detective. So, what happened next in this little story of yours?"

"Well, when I walked into the artist's studio, who, by the way, is named Gino Rispoli, I figured Rispoli might have heard something. Mr. Rispoli is a very colorful character. He wears bright, outlandish colors and outfits. But I was quite impressed by Mr. Rispoli's work. He told me that a few years ago in 1977, he had fallen on hard times and started making life-sized plaster nativity scenes for some Catholic churches and a few private homes on the Island. His scenes were so good that he was soon in demand. So, Mr. Rispoli spent more time making the nativity figures. He starts taking orders in July."

"Where does Mr. Rispoli fit into this case? Did the killer enter the studio? Did Rispoli witness something significant without even realizing it?"

"Mr. Gino Rispoli witnessed everything...because Mr. Gino Rispoli was the killer."

"What? How did you figure that out?"

"I'm not going to say it was easy. Because it wasn't, he probably would have gotten away with it if it hadn't been for the wig, the reflection on the glass, and the fact that I moved his statue."

"Elaborate, please."

"Riley Ackroyd described the killer he saw in the mirror. What he looked like. What he was wearing. And that he was holding the man he was choking in his left arm. Even the killer went to the desk and wrote something with his left hand."

"And it came to you that the reflection in the mirror would have it backward."

"Yes, that meant I was mistaken about the killer being lefthanded. If I was wrong about that, maybe everything else was wrong too. Maybe it was all a disguise. The killer was anxious for the window washer to see him. He didn't try to conceal his identity. Maybe there was a reason."

"So that takes care of the reflection in the glass, but you also mentioned a wig."

"When we came into Mr. Rispoli's studio, he was putting the finishing touches on a figure of one of the wise men. He was on a ladder affixing a wig and beard to the wise man's head, brown beard and brown hair pulled back into a ponytail. And he had a red sash tied around the waist."

"So, now you think you have the killer. Or at least a man who fits the window washer's description of the killer. The hair, the clothes, the beard...but you have no dead body."

"Oh, but we do...Mr. Rispoli was clever. When he called his former partner, who had absconded with all his money and left him so desperate that he needed to make nativity scenes to put bread on the table, he asked him to meet him early in the morning on the 17th floor using his own entrance code to enter.

'Wait…why not have his partner meet him in the basement? That would save a lot of time."

"When Rispoli confessed, he told us that he couldn't have his old partner meet him in the basement because the man would never have come. The man, Alfred Hamm, knew how angry Rispoli was and did not trust him enough to be lured into a dark basement. So, Rispoli had Hamm come upstairs. He waited for him inside Ms. Hernandez's office, and then he killed him. After transporting Hamm to his studio, he put his body in his plaster of Paris trough, coated it with the wet plaster, and when it was set enough, he put him in the wise man pose and let him dry completely. Rispoli is as strong as an ox. Plaster of Paris takes about 45 minutes to set. When the figure was dried, he stood him up among the rest of the nativity scenes and then painted him. Then he turned the red tie into a sash and put the wig and the beard on the plastered corpse."

"So how…you don't mean…?"

"Yes. When Rispoli left the room, I tried to push on the figure that Rispoli was working on, but it wouldn't budge. It was heavy. Then, I saw Rispoli moving one of the other figures with ease. So, I tried a few more of the statues, all of which were movable. That's when I realized where the body was hidden."

"What about Riley Ackroyd? Did you bring him down to I.D. Rispoli as the killer?"

"Yes. I did. Mr. Ackroyd was pretty shaken up when he saw the artist standing there. He knew he was staring at the killer. That was Rispoli's mistake. He came to the glass to taunt the window washer, thinking that the disguise was strong enough to hide his true identity. And since there were no windows in his basement studio, he figured the window washer would never see him again. But Ackroyd was close enough to get a good look. And down in that dark basement, he could see the man behind the disguise. The window washer was afraid I didn't believe him. But I told him that an eye witness' words were the only ones that convict."

"So, the body never left the building."

"No. It was there the whole time. Standing beside the manger with a sack of frankincense in its hand."

"It was the word of the window washer witness. He was the beginning, and he was the end. The evidence was in, and Rispoli was the verdict. Nice work, Detective Tracy."

Tracy smiled. "I think it was John Garfield in some movie noir who said with my brains and your looks, we could go places…"

WHAT THE BLIND MAN SAW

PROLOGUE

Miss Sadie Bloom sat straight up in her bed. "May the Irish saints preserve us." Sadie shouted as she sprang from beneath the covers and reached for her tattered bathrobe. She slid her feet into her worn pink slippers and dashed to her bedroom door. Sadie was certain the shots had come from the kitchen.

When she threw open the swinging door that led down the galley, the smell of gunpowder was still heavy in the air. Sadie considered screaming, but it would have been futile; no one would hear her; the family's private quarters in the great farmhouse were upstairs and at the far end. Gathering her strength with one deep breath, Sadie opened the kitchen door. What she saw terrified her. Without hesitation, the housekeeper turned and ran through the dining room, into the hallway, up the stairs, and down the long corridor that opened onto the master bedroom and the eight guest rooms.

Where should she knock first? That was Sadie's dilemma. She rapped on the master bedroom door.

"Mrs... Please open the door. Quickly. Something has happened." When she received no reply, Sadie knocked harder...and louder. "...Mrs. O'Connell, please open the door. It's Sadie. I need you. Hurry."

It took only seconds for a fuzzy-headed woman in her early fifties to open the door. Patsy Shannon O'Connell adjusted the belt of her housecoat.

"What is it Sadie? My God, it's two in the morning. You will wake our guests."

Too late to worry about that. Several doors were now thrown open, sleepy-eyed heads sticking out, and necks craning to see what all the commotion was about. "You have to come quickly, Mrs. It's your husband and his brother. There's been a horrible accident in the kitchen...oh, please hurry."

Patsy O'Connell ran for the stairs, almost overtaking the weeping Sadie, who was reciting her Hail-Marys as they ran. When the two women reached the kitchen, Patsy O'Connell pushed open the swinging door. What she saw was beyond words. On the floor, in pools of blood, lay her husband and his younger brother dressed in pajamas and robes. Milk and cookies spilled across the counter. To Patsy's eyes, there was no question that her husband, Warren O'Connell, was dead. The gaping head wound was no doubt fatal. His blind brother Bennett, younger by two years, was unmoving; the blood pooled around his leg and hip, but she could see Bennett's chest heaving up and down rapidly. He was alive.

Patsy's voice was calm and steady. She gave her loyal housekeeper orders. "Go into the study and call an ambulance on the second line, Sadie. I will call the police from line one here in the kitchen. And don't let anyone else pass through this door."

As her housekeeper left the kitchen, Patsy reached for the phone and dialed the operator. After completing her call, she bent down and tentatively touched her husband but hesitated. As much as she wanted to cradle him in her arms, she knew better. Nothing should be disturbed. Patsy O'Connell stood up and crossed the kitchen floor. It would be difficult to tell her two grown children that their father had passed away. And if Bennett, his brother, died too, she didn't want to think about all of that right now. She just wanted to get through the next few minutes. So, she pushed open the door only to find Sadie standing guard on the other side. Sadie stood with her arms crossed over her chest, while behind the housekeeper, the family members were gathered in various bedclothes. Patsy's eyes quickly scanned over the group. Was everyone here? No. Someone was missing—in fact, two someones. Patsy composed herself. She couldn't let her children see her fall apart.

"A tragedy occurred here tonight. Let's wait in the living room until the police and ambulance arrive. I will explain everything once we're settled in.

Patsy O'Connell led the way to the large wood-paneled room just to the left of the kitchen door. Solemnly, the other family members followed as if they were in a dream that would soon become... a nightmare.

* * *

*"The tongue may hide the truth,
but the eyes, never."*
-M. Bulgakov

The double doors were firmly closed once the weekend guests were comfortably settled in the farmhouse living room. Everyone remained in their nightclothes, wide-eyed and anxious. Some paced while others sat quietly like church mice, all waiting for Patsy to speak. A tragedy had occurred; that was all they knew. No one wanted to hear bad news.

Everyone had gathered three days earlier for an O'Connell family reunion. Each family member had brought a spouse or significant other, except for Father Flannigan. The group included the two adult O'Connell children. Warren's brother Bennett, a nephew, a niece, Patsy O'Connell's sister, and the family priest. They gathered for a magnificent weekend on the expansive farm, where the main house now looked like a gentleman's country estate. The original four-room farmhouse has undergone numerous renovations, evolving into a sprawling two-story structure that covers 10,000 square feet. It included eight bedrooms, ten bathrooms, a living room, a study, two offices, and a kitchen large enough to accommodate all the farmhands on Sunday mornings. The Pennsylvania farm had become the flagship of the O'Connell family's produce business, and last night, it hosted the family dinner, filled with delicious food, laughter, and moments of connection. And now this.

Patsy O'Connell could sense all eyes on her as she walked to the far side. As much as Patsy wanted to break down, she held it together. It fell upon her to deliver the horrible news. She had spared them the scene in the kitchen, the gruesome sight of their beloved family member dead... and perhaps his brother too. She began slowly. "I have had a terrible shock, everyone. My husband has been shot. He is in the kitchen. The ambulance and the police have been called..."

There was a collective gasp as Patsy's son, Michael, jumped to his feet. "Mother, what are you talking about? Why aren't we in there...?"

"Because, son...there is no easy way to say this; he is dead. There is no hope of revival, no hope whatsoever..."

The wail of an ambulance could be heard in the distance. No one moved; some were barely breathing. "I want everyone to remain downstairs until the police come. I'm sure they will want to talk to all of us. Especially you, Sadie...since you were the one who discovered the bodies."

"BODIES???" Peggy O'Connell Smith cried.

"Yes. Your uncle Bennett has been shot also, but he is still alive. Barely."

The sound of the ambulance coming to a screeching halt drew everyone's attention. Michael spoke with a force his mother had never experienced before. "I'm going into the kitchen, Mother... do not try and stop me. Sadie, go and let the paramedics in."

Father Gerald Flanagan, not a family member but a trusted part of their lives, jumped up from the couch to Patsy's right. "Let me go also, please. I must administer Last Rites. If Bennett is still alive..."

The view on the floor of the vast kitchen unsettled Michael O'Connell. He stifled a cry and then sobbed into his hand. He fell to his knees beside his father. Father Flanagan began administering the Last Rites over Bennett O'Connell. Both men stepped aside to give the now-present paramedics room to work.

The victims were quickly placed onto stretchers—a sheet covered Warren O'Connell, confirming his death—an IV tube extended from Bennett O'Connell's arm. As the team left, they passed by everyone now gathered at the front door. The women were shocked, their hands covering their mouths in disbelief, while the men appeared pale and shaken.

"I'm going with my husband's body and then to the hospital," Patsy informed the group. With that, she ran to get dressed. She heard the police being admitted as she rounded the second-floor landing. The local police department was not equipped to handle a homicide, and she wanted answers. Someone in this house had shot her husband and his brother. The only three people she felt that didn't fire that gun were her son, her daughter, and Father Gerald Flanagan. Patsy O'Connell had already decided to call an old friend who knew her when she was still Patsy Shannon- a man who, over the years, had become a friend to the O'Connell family. He was a New York City homicide detective named Nick Tracy.

***

"There are some things that can only be seen thru eyes that have cried."
- O. Romero

NYPD Detective Nicholas Tracy was welcomed at the door by Miss Sadie Bloom. Despite her sadness, she appeared pleased to see him. It had been far too long between visits. Aside from a brief overnight stay for the recent wedding, it had been years since Tracy had visited for any meaningful duration. She took his coat and then motioned for him to follow. "Come on, Nicky. Everyone's upstairs, napping and getting ready for the wake. None of us have had much sleep in the last two days. I hope you'll stay."

Tracy smiled. Staying was precisely what he had in mind. "Yes, thank you, Sadie."

"Okay. Please make yourself at home in the living room, and you know where it is. I'll let the Mrs. know. Give me your suitcase, and I will put it in the Elk Bedroom. Then I'll make sure the sheets are clean for 'ya.' It's good to have you here. It's been horrible. I'm the one who discovered the bodies, you know." With that, Sadie made the sign of the cross and then scurried away.

Tracy walked through the hall into the spacious living room and settled into an overstuffed chair by the window. He looked up at the taxidermy animal heads decorating the wall. Whenever he visited the farm, he felt uneasy in that room, as if the marble eyes were watching him. He felt a constant urge to apologize to the heads. Tracy shook off the sensation.

Patsy filled him in on a few details regarding her husband's shooting. Tracy liked and admired Warren O'Connell. He was a regular kind of guy. He had continued in his father's footsteps, making even more money than the old man in the Pennsylvania produce business. Tracy was startled by the sudden sound of voices. He heard the two people enter the room before they realized they were not alone. The woman spoke sternly. "...and I don't understand this wake business. In my country we do not do such things."

Kenneth O'Connell, Patsy's nephew, paused as he suddenly sensed another presence in the room. When he realized who it was, he brightened. His shoulders returned to their natural position, and he stood taller. "Hello, Nick. I haven't seen you in ages. I think you know my wife, Natasha."

Detective Tracy nodded in the direction of the Russian Greta Garbo. *Stop it!* Tracy said to himself. Putting movie star tags on people had finally become an annoying habit. But not one easily broken.

"Yes, we've met. How are you, Natasha?"

Tracy received nothing more than a simple head nod as the couple sank into the chenille sofa, waiting for the others to join them. Tracy tried to make small talk, but it was not reciprocated, leaving them in silence. Shortly afterward, the door swung open, revealing three couples followed by a handsome man in late middle age wearing a priest's collar. Introductions were unnecessary.

It was Michael O'Connell and his wife, Jennifer Costas O'Connell. The daughter, Peggy O'Connell Smith, and her husband, James Smith. Also present were Barbara Finley, a niece of the O'Connells, and her latest intended victim, Mr. Forest Carlysle. He appeared to be a younger specimen of manhood than the previous men Ms. Finley had introduced. Also present was Father Gerald Flanagan. Stiff pleasantries were exchanged. Father Flanagan was the first to approach; the mark of the Irish graced his ruddy, dimpled cheeks. "So good to see you, Nick. All we can do at this time is offer condolences and comfort."

"Yes, Father. Patsy was brief on the phone, so I stopped by the local police station to read the reports and statements from everyone here that night, but I feel like something is missing."

"It was all very sad, Nick. Sadie heard the shots from her bedroom, came into the kitchen, found the two bodies, and then woke everyone up. After the police came, we were each interviewed separately. I understand they even questioned the ranch hands who were in the bunkhouse. The officers left with a warning not to leave town, and they came back the following morning with a few more questions, and that was it. We are all being allowed to go home as soon as the funeral is over tomorrow."

"And what is your take on all of this, Father? The police have ruled out an intruder."

"I wish I could be of more help, but you know that no one here is a killer. From what I gather, the investigating officer located the gun in the kitchen pantry. I heard it belonged to Warren. However, on a more positive note, Warren's brother Bennett is expected to survive, which must be difficult for a man who is blind."

Father Flanagan moved away without another word as Tracy consulted his list of notes, most taken from the local police report. There wasn't much to go on.

* * *

"Almost nothing need be said...
when you have eyes."
-T. Vesaas

Detective Tracy entered the hospital through the revolving doors. After revealing his badge, he was escorted to Mr. Bennett O'Connell's room on the second floor. As Tracy recalled, the middle-aged man had the appearance of an Irish barkeep. His face was round and jovial. He could easily pass for Carroll O'Connor. He was sitting up, slightly sedated from pain medication, yet alert. His injuries had been treated, and the doctors had approved visitors.

When Tracy introduced himself to the blind man, Bennett O'Connell immediately recognized the name. He was warm and receptive, expressing his profound sorrow for not being able to attend his brother's burial. He swiftly regained his composure. "Please sit down, Nick. Is there a chair nearby? I can answer any questions you have. Patsy told me to expect you. I gave the police my account of the events from that night; I'm sure you saw the report. I'm unsure if I can provide additional help from this hospital bed, but I'll try."

"Thank you, Mr. O'Connell."

"Oh, please. If I'm going to call you Nick, the least you can do is call me Bennett."

Tracy seated himself comfortably on a side chair placed by the bed. "Ok, Bennett. I read the report, but if you don't mind, sir, please tell me exactly what you remember about that night. Starting with the moment you entered the kitchen."

"This will be short and sweet Nick... I couldn't sleep; there had been a party that evening at the farmhouse, and I guess my adrenaline was flowing. I knew Warren would be up; he's a terrible sleeper, always has been, even as a kid. Our parents didn't know it, but we spent half the night under the covers reading comic books. I had my sight back in those days."

Bennett O'Connell shifted in the bed before continuing. "...I heard my brother pouring his milk when I entered the kitchen. I could even smell Sadie's cookies; they were left over from the party—peanut butter with chocolate chips. Warren had me sit on a stool while he poured me a glass of milk. And before he could finish, the door to the kitchen swung open, and someone entered."

"I read in the report that your brother addressed the person."

"Yes. He said something like, 'Oh, I see you couldn't sleep either; I guess that's understandable.' And then there was a loud shot, then a second shot. I stood... I tried to run, but in my haste, I ran in the wrong direction. I ran AT the killer and not away. Within a matter of moments, I felt the bullet strike my side. Whoever fired the gun was very close to me. I heard the kitchen door swinging closed as I fell to the floor. When I came to myself, I was in an ambulance on the way here, to the hospital."

"And there's nothing else you can tell me about that night?"

"No. The person who tried to kill us both didn't say a word. But I do remember that whoever fired that gun was wearing street shoes. Not bedroom slippers, as you would expect at two in the morning. And one of the shoes was missing a tap. The two shoes didn't make the same sound. And...I think I may have a way to identify the killer if I can get out of this bed. I would need to have everyone there."

"What do you have in mind, sir?"

"I don't want to say what I'm thinking, Nick. It might not work. But I'm willing to try."

Detective Tracy gathered up his notes. This request from the blind man reminded him of a recent case.

"I can provide you with that opportunity sir...I will ask Patsy to invite everyone back to the farmhouse to welcome you home. Who could refuse?"

Tracy stopped to make a few scribbles in his notebook. Bennet O'Connell must have heard the sound of the pen because he remained silent: **Street shoes, one tap missing. The killer didn't speak.**

Tracy rose to leave. After a handshake and an expression of gratitude, the detective moved towards the door. Behind his back, he heard Bennett O'Connell's parting words. "Whoever did this, Nick, they feel they are safe. Let them. What killer would be afraid of a blind man?"

* * *
"Curiosity is gluttony. To see is to devour."
-V. Hugo

There was a service, a mass, and a few eulogies read. It was brief, just the way Warren O'Connell would have wanted. After the graveside burial, everyone was due back at the O'Connell farm for an after-funeral buffet. Tracy followed in his car. Some farmhands were doubling as valets, standing at the ready, parking everyone's car quietly. Tracy entered the front door, following behind everyone else. He wouldn't admit it out of respect for the deceased, but Tracy was not there for social pleasantries. He was there to find a killer. And to do that, he needed to ask questions.

The first person he approached was the O'Connell family heir standing alone with a drink by the living room fireplace. Michael O'Connell was tall, lanky, and dignified. Tracy thought of Cary Grant immediately. "Lawyer" was written all over his face, clothes, and telltale courtroom stance. He had made his father proud by attending law school and passing the bar on his first try, but underneath it all, Tracy knew that Warren had regretted his only son would not be managing the farms.

"I want to offer my condolences, Michael. I had a great deal of respect for your father. I admired him."

"Thank you, Nick. He felt the same about you. I hope you can assist the local police in finding his killer."

"If you don't mind, I do have a few questions. But if now is not the time..."

"No. Please ask."

"What do you think about all of this? The police are nowhere near making an arrest."

A slight gesture, a rub of his hand over his face, indicated to Tracy that Michael O'Connell was uncomfortable. He was accustomed to asking the questions. "I don't know. Of the family members, there isn't one person in this house that didn't love my father. I can't personally vouch for others outside the family...I mean, I don't know anything about this man, this Forrest Carlisle, that my cousin brought for the weekend. He is a bit curious and doesn't have much to say. I would venture to guess that the French accent is fake. His hands are too soft for manual labor. And what's with that thick gold chain around his neck? He keeps it tucked in his shirt, so I haven't seen what's hanging from it. And as far as cousins go, Barbara Finley is somewhat of a black sheep in the family. She goes through men like water. I can't imagine Barbara, or this Carlisle would have anything to gain by killing my father or Uncle Bennett. Can you check into his background?"

"I plan on doing just that. He's the only one here that no one had met before a few days ago."

"Other than that, I don't know... Oh, here's my wife, Jennifer... I still can't get used to saying, 'My wife.' Maybe she can help. She is the most observant person I've ever known."

Detective Tracy turned and came face to face with Jennifer Costas O'Connell. The raven-haired beauty looked just as Tracy remembered her from the wedding.

"Hello, Mrs. O'Connell. It's nice to see you. I'm still finding rice in my hair from your beautiful wedding. I'm sorry we have to meet again under such sad circumstances."

Michael O'Connell's wife smiled brightly and almost as quickly removed the smile from her lips. "Yes, Nick. It's a sad day. Michael tells me you hope to help the police find the killer."

Tracy glanced over the young wife's shoulder. The deer heads seemed to be staring at him as if they, too, were waiting for his answer. "I am going to try. I've asked your husband if he remembers anything from that night that might help. If I may, I'd like to ask you the same question. There was a party earlier in the evening?"

"It was a wonderful celebration. We played quite an amusing game after dinner. I believe Father Flannigan, the priest, recommended it."

"Who won the game?"

"I believe it was Michael's Aunt Pamela. But honestly, I'm not sure."

Michael O'Connell grabbed for his wife's arm. "I'm sure Nick doesn't want to hear about some silly game, Jen." He seemed to be suddenly on edge.

"Oh, but I do, Michael," Tracy corrected. "What was the name of this game?"

Jennifer O'Connell straightened her black dress and disengaged her husband's hand. "Let me think…Oh yes, Spill the Beans. You had to tell something about the person sitting on your left. If you didn't know the person on your left, you had to get up and change seats to sit on the right of someone you knew. Which, of course, changed the dynamics of the table. It was fun."

"Were there any surprises? Michael tells me that you are very observant, Mrs. O'Connell."

"The secrets were quite mundane, Detective. There were a couple of old teenage incidents: a fistfight, a girl who didn't see eye to eye, a silly peeping Tom thing, a joy ride with Daddy's car, a missing statue, and an incident involving Patsy and Pamela switching places on their double dates... those sorts of things."

"What about at dinner? Did anyone argue or exchange cross words?"

"I thought Michael's cousin, Kenneth, was a bit standoffish. I understand he's a doctor."

Tracy nodded, not fully grasping the meaning of Jennifer O'Connell's observations. He excused himself and crossed the room to make a few entries in his book: **Michael O'Connell doesn't know anything about Forrest Carlisle. Daughter-in-law Jennifer O'Connell says cousin Kenneth O'Connell was quiet.**

* * *

"You believe what your eyes want to believe."
-S. Kalwar

Tracy put away his notebook and crossed the room once more. He approached the attractive woman and her male companion, a man considerably younger. The woman was tall, willowy, and over-dressed for the wood-paneled room. As Michael O'Connell had put it, Barbara Finley was the black sheep of the family. A very glamorous and wealthy black sheep who resembled Bette Davis in her prime. Tracy cleared his throat loudly before speaking. "Excuse me...my name is Nicholas Tracy. An old friend of the family."

The two heads that had been close together in quiet conversation parted abruptly and turned. *Nothing to say?* Tracy thought to himself as he continued. "...Patsy and I have been friends for many years. I was told you are Barbara Finley, a niece by marriage. Patsy has asked me to assist in the investigation."

"No need to list your credentials, I know who you are, Nick. I inquired about you last night at the wake. Patsy filled me in. This whole thing is ghastly. So, what can Forrest and I do for you?"

Tracy's detective side began a line of questioning.

"I wonder if either of you noticed anything unusual the night of the party. Did anyone threaten either brother? Did you overhear any hostile conversations?"

"No, I didn't hear anything. Except for that silly game we played, most of the night was spent in peace."

"What do you mean 'except for the game'? Did something happen during the game?"

"Not really. It started simple enough, but the tempers got a bit testy with the musical chairs. Most of the stuff people said was probably made up. Do you think that's important, Detective?"

"I don't think so. Parlor games rarely lead to murder. Was everyone in the room playing the game?"

"No. There were only twelve of us. Kenneth's Russian mail-order-bride begged off."

"Everyone else was in the room?"

"Yes. Except... I remember that Pamela Shannon, Patsy's twin sister, often left the room. One pretext after another. Like she was making up excuses as she went along. Some were borderline silly."

"Such as?"

"She had to make a call to her hairdresser... really? Who makes appointments on a Friday night at 8 o'clock? But other than Pamela, everyone else remained in the room."

"Where was Miss Sadie Bloom, the housekeeper?"

"Oh, Sadie was keeping the snack tray full, restocking the liquor, and running for items here and there. And if you're thinking that Sadie might be the one to shoot those two old geezers, Detective, think again. She is as loyal as they come. She wouldn't shoot anyone unless they threatened to shoot her first."

"I think I agree with you. And I believe the police agree with both of us. Sadie is not in consideration."

"Well, then, who are you considering, Detective? One of the farmhands?" It was the first time Forrest Carlisle had spoken. He looked like he was running out of whatever charm he once had.

"I haven't drawn any conclusions, Mr. Carlisle. I would say that everyone at the farm that night is a suspect. There's a motive behind that, I'm certain. I will uncover it. Someone wanted these two men dead." With that, Detective Tracy turned his back and went through the living room door. He found the powder room unoccupied and went in. After closing and locking the door, he made a few notes: **Kenneth O'Connell's wife, Natasha, was not in the room during the game. Barbara Finley says that Pamela Shannon, Patsy's twin sister, left the room often for trumped-up reasons.**

***

"The eyes are not responsible when the mind does the seeing."- P. Syrus

The next individual on Detective Tracy's list was Kenneth O'Connell and his wife Natasha, who sat together on the overstuffed velvet sofa in the corner of the room. Neither spoke to anyone nor each other. Tracy approached slowly. "Excuse me, Dr. O'Connell. Do you and your wife have a few minutes?"

Kenneth O'Connell looked up with only his eyes. His wife didn't bother. "Sure, Nick. Why don't you pull up a chair?"

Detective Tracy did so without being asked twice. "I'm sorry to intrude on your privacy, but I wonder...do you know why anyone in the house that night would want to shoot Warren and Bennett O'Connell?"

Tracy had addressed the question directly to Kenneth O'Connell. But his wife Natasha answered. "I know nothing."

Tracy repeated the question. Kenneth O'Connell, a brooding man with steely eyes, withdrew a pipe from his pocket and placed the stem between his teeth. "If you want me to name a suspect on which to pin this case, Nick, you've got the wrong man..."

Dr. Kenneth O'Connell saw the value in being direct. "...Why not begin with Uncle Warren's will if you are searching for a motive? Speak to his son. Michael knows who stands to gain from Uncle Warren's death. Money is always the answer, isn't it, Detective? And as far as his brother Bennett...my guess is that he was in the way. Just happened to be in the kitchen at the time."

"I'm sure you are right about Bennett O'Connell. He was in the wrong place at the wrong time. And as far as the money aspect goes, money isn't always the motive, Doctor.

I'm sure you want to see your uncle's killer caught just as much as everyone else."

Natasha seemed to have suddenly recovered her grasp of the English language. The heavy-set, dark-haired woman didn't wait to be asked. "I tell you that priest, he has bad karma. Look at the priest, Detective. I'm telling you, look very close at the priest."

Tracy nodded toward the dramatic Garbo-esque Russian, and then left the brooding couple to stand by the fireplace. He leaned against the mantle and made a few notes in his book: ***Kenneth says to check with Michael on the will. Who stands to benefit from Warren O'Connell's death? Natasha says Father Flanagan has bad karma. Does he?***

As he finished his last note, Tracy heard it. Distinctively. He would never have noticed the sound if the blind man hadn't alerted him. It was the uneven sound of a man's shoe on the wooden floor, barely audible over the din of conversation— one shoe with a tap, the other without. But it didn't matter because a missing tap wasn't enough evidence to convict a man of murder.

* * *

"When the tongue lies, the eyes tell the truth."
-G.H. Lorimer

Father Gerald Flanagan was over by the buffet table, helping himself. He didn't see Tracy coming. He jumped when the detective addressed him. "Oh, Nick. You startled me. Give me a minute and I will join you."

The good Father hastily put his plate down, marked his place by tilting the back of the chair until it was resting on the edge of the table, (the way they did at parish dinners and Bingo games), and then crossed to stand with Tracy in the corner, beneath the stuffed head of a frightened looking deer. "What can I do for you, Nick?"

Tracy smiled. Natasha's assessment of good or bad karma aside, Father Flanagan was an absolute joy. "I'm just wondering, Father, if you recall anything about that night. For example, you suggested a game, Spill the Beans. Did anyone get angry? Did Bennett or Warren reveal someone's secret?"

"You know it's funny you say that, Nick. I think Warren told a story about his daughter Peggy and how she had taken a joy ride in one of the new tractors as a teenager. Something about causing an accident. Of course, that's a story you could hear from the lips of every father in America. Teens can't seem to help themselves when first experimenting behind the wheel."

"Switching it around, did anyone tell a story about Warren?"

"Yes... I think someone told a story about Warren being a peeping Tom when he was a kid. Another incident that could be said about every boy hitting puberty. Boys go through those stages. You would be surprised at what I hear in the confessional box. Joy rides and peeping Tom stories are the norm."

"Okay. Sounds like pretty harmless stuff. Now, what about Mr. Bennett O'Connell?"

"Well, let's see. I think Bennett told a story about his nephew Michael. Apparently, Michael had confided in him about a girl in high school whom he had a crush on. There was an altercation at a party, and Michael came home with a black eye. I don't think Michael minded when his uncle told the story; he laughed along with the rest of us.

"Thank you, Father. If you think of anything else, I need to know, please call me."

Tracy made a note in his book as he walked away: ***The story was told during game time that Warren was caught, a peeping Tom. Bennett told the story about Michael and the girl he couldn't get over. He was in a fight. Was someone seriously injured in this fight?***

* * *

*"Fix your eyes on what you believe.
Not what you see."*
-C. Burkmenn

Pamela Shannon commanded attention. The lively woman's audience included several funeral attendees gathered at the makeshift bar against the living room's back wall. Patsy O'Connell's unmarried twin sister had many stories about Warren. Some members of her audience were genuinely interested, while others were just being polite. Yet, no one made a move to leave. Perhaps the tray of liquor was the adhesive keeping them all together. Tracy stood at the edge of the group, waiting for a pause in Pamela's narratives. Would it ever come? When he finally saw his opportunity, he took it. "Miss Shannon. May I speak to you, please?"

Pamela waved her hand in the air like the Queen herself as a farewell to those gathered and followed Tracy to an open area against the near wall. When she extended her hand in greeting, Tracy grabbed for the soft white skin, and soon, his own was lost in a crush of assorted rings. "It's nice to see you again, Nick. Just call me Pamela. It's been quite a while. I wish it were under better circumstances, but there's no avoiding this unpleasant situation with Warren and Bennett."

"I'm glad to hear you say that, Pamela. I wonder if you could think back to that night?"

"Nothing happened, Nick, that I'm aware of. And please don't ask me to nod in the direction of someone I suspect would do such a thing. The whole experience is almost too dreadful to recall, and as much as I want to, I can't get one second of it out of my mind."

"Why don't you give me your account, starting with the events before you went to bed."

Pamela Shannon nodded. Her gestures and demeanor echoed like Judy Garland performing on an empty stage. After staring into imaginary space, she slowly transformed into a woman with remarkable recall. "I went to bed and slept soundly until about 2:20. Noticing the clock on my nightstand, I then heard Sadie screaming outside Patsy's room. That's when I picked up my robe from the floor and came down the stairs."

"Who did you see coming downstairs with you?"

"Everyone, except Father Flanagan and Kenneth. Patsy was already in the kitchen. When she came out, she told us what happened, and we all waited for the police and ambulance to arrive."

"You mentioned Father Flanagan and Kenneth O'Connell were not part of the group that arrived immediately. How long was it before they joined the rest of you?"

"Maybe five minutes. It felt like time had stopped, making everything move slowly. It was like a bad dream from which your mind refuses to wake up. I can't say for certain. But it couldn't have been less than five minutes, and it may have been more."

"And what excuse did they give?"

"When Sadie went back upstairs to wake them, Father Flanagan said he hadn't heard anything because he had been sleeping with earplugs and that his own snoring would wake him up if he didn't. Kenneth didn't give an excuse. He just turned to his wife and asked her why she didn't wake him when she heard the commotion. Natasha of course said very little. She failed to offer any explanation."

"And what do you think of all this? Who do you think wanted harm to come to Bennett and Warren?"

"I don't know for sure, Nick. But we know very little about Jennifer Costas; she has only been an O'Connell for a short time. And..." Pamela Shannon cupped her hand around her mouth and lowered her voice. "... I understand her father has mob connections. The Costas family doesn't have a very good reputation. Maybe Warren had dealings with them in the produce business..." Pamela removed her cupped hand and resumed her normal speaking voice. "... and who knows anything about this Forrest Carlisle character that Barbara showed up with."

"Okay, thank you, Pamela. I will let you go back to your friends now."

Pamela Shannon kissed Tracy's cheek and then crossed the room. Behind her back, Detective Tracy was already busy writing: **Kenneth O'Connell and Father Flanagan were five minutes late coming downstairs after the shooting. Where were they? Father Flanagan had an excuse, but Kenneth did not. Did the Russian wife fail to wake Kenneth because she wasn't in the room? If not, where was she?**

* * *

"Eyes. They watch and make notes."
-A. Chekhov

When Detective Tracy went to seek out Peggy O'Connell Smith, he was informed that the O'Connell daughter was lying upstairs. Tracy sought the next best thing: her husband. James Smith was staring out the large picture window as Tracy stepped up. "I'm sorry to bother you, James. But if you wouldn't mind answering a few questions."

James Smith turned. He squared his shoulders and stood at military attention. James had a leading man face that was now swollen and red. It appeared he had foregone a shave that morning. Tracy knew that Warren O'Connell's son-in-law had worked for Warren in the produce business since marrying Peggy. Someday, this farm and the business would belong to Peggy and James and their children. "I noticed you were making the rounds, Nick. I suppose it's my turn in the crosshairs. I'm very willing to help in any way that I can. Peggy is almost inconsolable. I'm doing my best to hold up my end. Do I get a cigarette and a blindfold? If not, fire away."

"I understand that Warren had some labor disputes. Could this shooting have anything to do with… "

"No, Nick. The problems have all cleared up. Warren felt as if we were back on the right track."

"Okay. Then what do you remember about the party?"

"There was nothing unusual. Honestly, I can't imagine why anyone would go to the extreme of killing Warren and then turning the gun on Bennett. Have you received any help from the others?"

"Everyone says the same thing. There was never a reason to kill Warren or Bennett." Tracy's eyes met James Smith's in an official capacity. "... Of course, someone is lying."

If Tracy were waiting for a big telltale reaction, he would be disappointed. James Smith took a shallow breath and then did a half-turn so he was no longer directly facing Tracy. "Yes, I suppose someone is lying, Nick. And what about the gun? The murder weapon?"

"It was one of Warren's own. No fingerprints. No help."

"One of Warren's?" Smith repeated. "What are you going to do about the ... oh, wait a moment, I see Peggy entering the room. I'm sure you'll want to talk to her, but promise you won't upset her."

When James Smith crossed the room to retrieve his wife, Tracy reminded himself to add a few words to his notebook. It was something that Smith had said...what was it? Oh, yes: ***How did he know that Warren was shot first, and then the shooter turned the gun on Bennett? Only the killer would know that piece of information. Unless someone else told him… and if so, who? The man with the missing tap on his shoe?***

*　*　*

*"The eyes see only what the mind
is prepared to comprehend."*
-R. Davies

Peggy O'Connell Smith was struggling deeply with her father's death. Her grief and sorrow were visible on her face. It would take some time for Warren O'Connell's daughter to recover from the shock. Detective Tracy observed as the young woman he had known since childhood approached. He had visions in his head: a little red-haired imp climbing up into the barn rafters covered in hay...the first day of kindergarten...a high school cap and gown...a wedding... a couple of births. It all came flooding back as he watched her weave through the vast room, saying very little to anyone. When she was at last standing by his side, Tracy was thinking... this young woman could have been my daughter. "I . . I'm so sorry, Peggy...I . . I...can't tell you how much."

Peggy O'Connell Smith threw her arms around her longtime confidante. At that moment he was Nick Tracy, family friend, and not the detective trying to find the man who killed her father. "Oh, Nicky. I can't believe this. It's all so awful. Who would want to kill Daddy? Everyone loved him."

Tracy kept his arms around the slender redhead's shoulders. He pulled her closer. "I don't know Peg, but I'm going to find out what happened. I promise I will find the truth."

Peggy stepped out of Tracy's arms. "Truth, Nicky? Really?" She turned to look around the room, not really seeing. "... I know you're going to ask me if I remember anything about that night. But I can honestly tell you that nothing happened. Whatever caused someone to shoot Father and Uncle Bennett, it must have been brewing from the past. It can't be business. Uncle Bennett has nothing to do with Daddy's business. If someone wanted both brothers out of the way, it wasn't over union money."

Tracy felt a pang of guilt for bothering the distraught redhead at such a delicate time. He didn't want to keep her any longer than necessary. He gave her a light kiss on the cheek. "Go and be with your husband and family. I will keep you posted on anything I come up with."

Peggy nodded absent-mindedly and wandered away. Tracy knew his next order of business would not be pleasant. He had to talk to Patsy O'Connell. His eyes searched the room. The grieving widow sat by the fireplace, surrounded by family. When she caught Tracy looking her way, she gestured toward the door. They met almost simultaneously and exited the room together, hand in hand.

***

"A woman's eyes cut deeper than a knife."
-R. Jordan

Nick Tracy and Patsy O'Connell entered the study that had been so much a part of Warren O'Connell's life. His stamp was everywhere. His books, his artifacts, his photos, even his papers on the desk. The only thing missing from the room was the gun that had killed him. Sensing the first order of business, Patsy inclined her head toward the large chest of drawers inherited with the farmhouse. "The gun was kept in that top drawer. So, the grandchildren couldn't possibly reach it. Not all the members of the family knew it was there."

"Who did know?"

"Oh, all the men: Michael, Kenneth, Bennett, James, and probably Father Flanagan. You know how Warren liked to talk. The gun had no history. He bought it for protection. Did you know about it?"

Tracy nodded in the affirmative.

"Well, there you go, Nick. See? Warren liked to talk."

"How about the bullets? Who knew where those were kept?"

"Same people."

"Ok. And just so you know... I read in the police report that there were no traces of residue on anyone except the victims. Of course, everyone would have had time to wash before and I know it looks like it had to be one of the men who knew about the gun but that doesn't exclude the women..."

"That's ridiculous, Nick. You're talking about Peggy, Natasha, and my new daughter-in-law, and..."

"How much do you know about Jennifer?"

"I know she is a sweet, loving girl. But beyond that…"

"Did you know that there are rumors about her father being in the mob? It seems far-fetched to me, but we can't rule out anything now. Or anyone. Friends come and go, but enemies accumulate."

"I suppose we can't rule out Pamela or Barbara either. My sister, my niece. It's all so utterly ridiculous that the killer could be one of the family members. What motive would any of them have for trying to kill Warren and Bennett? There must have been someone else in this house that night."

"What about Sadie? Are we sure she didn't let anyone else through her back entrance?"

"No. Sadie was not entertaining. Of that I'm sure."

"Does someone else have a key to this house?"

"Yes. The kids, Michael and Peggy... and my sister Pamela. Oh, and the ranch foreman."

"I will speak to him. When is Michael reading the will?"

"In two days." Patsy O'Connell looked away and then back again. Like a movie heroine. "Will you be present at the reading of Warren's will?"

"Of course. If you want me to."

"Yes, Nick. I think you should be there."

"Okay. I will be here. So that you know, not a single person believes a family member could have done this. That leaves Forrest Carlisle or Father Flanagan. I think it's unlikely that it would be someone from outside. Unless a family member let in someone they are seeing..."

"Do you mean like having an affair?"

"Maybe."

"Okay, Nick. Let's leave it at that. After the will is read, everyone is going home. Bennett, however, is going to stay here for a rest. I've hired a nurse to help out. He needs to get stronger." And with that Patsy O'Connell left the library. Tracy watched after his friend, who was still as beautiful as the day he had met her. At one point, he had envied Warren O'Connell. The king of the produce world had the girl he wished were his own. Through the years, Tracy had gotten over the envy and settled for friendship.

A few minutes later, when he felt it appropriate, Tracy snuck out to his waiting car. Later he added a few lines in his notebook: ***Outside key. Check with the foreman. Any farm workers have a key? Did they have access to the foreman's key? Do any of the workers have a reason to want Warren or Bennett dead? Gun kept in Warren's study. Men knew where. Did any of them share the information with their women***?

* * *

"Tears. The eyes are better for having been washed by them."
-C.N. Bovee

The reading of the will went off without a hitch. Everything was as it should have been. Warren O'Connell left the bulk of his estate to his wife and children. There was an allocated amount for his nephew, niece, and brother and a small sum for his ranch hands. The produce business was to be run by his son-in-law, James Smith. There was even a few thousand dollars for Father Gerald Flanagan's parish. Neat and tidy. There were no surprising codicils, nothing unexpected or shocking. Everyone was satisfied.

After the will was read, everyone gathered in the living room. Suitcases had been moved to the cars, and travel plans had been made. There was no need for airlines; everyone was just a train ride or car trip away from home. The police seemed satisfied that the investigation was progressing. They gave everyone the go-ahead to leave but added a strict, unnecessary warning against leaving the country.

Bennett O'Connell had returned from the hospital, and now a pair of crutches replaced his red-tipped cane. He looked as well as could be expected. Everyone had welcomed him with open arms and well wishes. He was staying in his usual room upstairs, and the hired nurse was next to him. A few family members expressed concern that the killer might come back. Although the exterior locks were replaced after the shooting, Patsy added new locks to the bedroom doors for herself and Bennett. She believed they would sleep better, and she was right.

As everyone gathered to leave, Detective Tracy pulled Bennett O'Connell aside and spoke to the blind man in a low voice. "You told me you might have a way to identify the killer, sir. And that you needed everyone present."

"Yes, Nick. I have already begun. It may not work, but I am going to attempt it. When everyone has departed, I will give you my impressions if you stick around."

Detective Tracy watched as the blind man picked his way through the gathered people, one by one. There didn't seem to be any method to the man's movement, but Tracy knew what wasn't apparent to him spoke volumes to a blind man. Everyone was cooperating without knowing they were. And later that night, when Tracy, Patsy, and Bennett were alone, Tracy knew he had been right to give the blind man free rein. Tracy was astonished when he heard the results of Bennett O'Connor's experiment. If Bennet O'Connell was right, the killer had executed everything with precision. It was nearly perfect.

The killer's mistake was underestimating a blind man. As Bennett O'Connell pointed out… "a man doesn't always need eyes to see."

* * *

"The world exists only in our eyes."
-F.S. Fitzgerald

It had only been a few days since the family's departure; most had scarcely had time to unpack, yet Patsy requested that everyone return for one night. The invitations read: *Your presence is requested for a quiet dinner in honor of B. O'Connell and his continued recovery. RSVP*

There were none among them who could refuse. Days later, everyone had arrived at the appointed time. Cocktails were served in the living room. Even with the lingering sadness, everyone seemed to be allowing themselves to enjoy the company. Of course, they had no idea what was coming. Soon, dinner was served—a catered feast, Italian style. When the dishes had been removed, and the caterers had cleared out, Detective Tracy asked everyone to join him in the kitchen.

Sideway glances were exchanged among those gathered. As each person entered the enormous galley kitchen, Patsy's daughter Peggy arrived, leading her uncle Bennett to the counter. He slid onto the stool he had occupied the night of the shooting, leaning his crutches against the edge. The assembled group turned to Tracy with anticipation, waiting.

"Thank you everyone. This has been a rough few weeks for all of you and me as I was asked to find a killer in a family that I love. Where do I start? When you all arrived that first night, there were no indications that anyone in this room had a reason to want to harm Bennett or Warren O'Connell. But something changed that night..."

Tracy pointed to Bennett O'Connell, who was sitting on the counter stool to his left. "This entire case hinged on the recollection of a blind man. The killer, as we know, shot Warren O'Connell first right in this very spot. Bennett heard the two shots. His instinct told him to get out. But he made the mistake of running towards the killer, not away. It's what saved his life. In doing so he knocked the gun downward, causing the two bullets to strike him in the leg and not higher. There were only four bullets in the gun because that's all Warren had in the house. And I'm guessing the killer didn't anticipate needing anymore because he wasn't expecting anyone to be here with Warren. So, he wiped the gun as clean as he could, threw it into the pantry, and fled upstairs to remove any gunshot residue."

Tracy walked over to where Sadie Bloom stood, looking shaken by the recollection of that night. "Sadie was the first on the scene..."

Tracy then strolled over to where Warren O'Connell's widow stood. "... Sadie then alerted Patsy, who arrived here in the kitchen, followed by everyone else except... Father Flanagan and Kenneth O'Connell. Patsy thought it strange they weren't with the group but didn't say anything until later."

Next, Tracy moved to the far side of the long counter. "... As I stated, this entire case rested on the memory of a blind man. Bennett remembered two things that night. One was the sound of street shoes on the kitchen floor, not the slippers that were expected. And not just street shoes but street shoes that were missing a tap on one heel. At first, I wasn't sure his memory was that good until I heard the sound myself, on the living room's wooden floor."

Next, Tracy moved over to the swinging door. "Also, when the killer entered the kitchen through this door, and before the gun was fired, there were a few moments when Warren was speaking to whoever had entered the room. He said, "I see you couldn't sleep, either. That's understandable." This indicated to me that Warren knew something had upset this person. It wouldn't have happened during dinner, as everyone assured me no crosswords were exchanged. Therefore, it must have occurred during the game played later in the evening..."

Tracy turned and approached Father Flanagan, who looked a bit flustered. "What was the game that you had suggested, Father?"

"Spill the Beans, it's called. We play it at the parish, sometimes. You tell something..."

"A secret?"

"Sure, if you want to. But nothing too harsh. It wouldn't be fun, then."

"What happens if you don't know anything about the person sitting on your right?"

"Then you move around the table, so you sit next to someone you DID know something about."

"And that's what happened that night. The person to the killer's left moved everyone around the table to sit and tell a story about him. A story that had been told with only half the truth. But a half-truth is a whole lie. There was an accident a few years ago..."

Kenneth O'Connell suddenly wheeled around to face Tracy. "Wait a minute, Nick. That accident story was about me. But Warren didn't tell the story."

"No, doctor, your cousin did. The moment she finished, you must have realized that Warren was the only one in the room who knew the truth. Am I right?"

"Yes but..."

"Someone may have put two and two together, and you couldn't have that. The other day, at the funeral, I heard you were missing a tap on your shoe. May I see the bottoms?"

Kenneth O'Connell turned over first one foot and then the other. One tap on and one tap gone.

"Look, Nick...I don't know what's going on here…come on everyone..."

Tracy talked over the doctor. "The final piece of the puzzle that fell into place was apparent to the keen senses of a blind man. Bennett walked around the living room the day before everyone left to make sure he wasn't mistaken. He stopped when he knew he had the killer. It was the smell. The smell of his cologne. The same smell from the night in the kitchen before the shots were fired." Tracy took a breath. "...And it was yours, doctor."

Kenneth O'Connell sputtered, caught off guard. "This is absurd."

"No, it's not. Being a doctor, you know a blind man's senses are heightened. You could have walked out of that kitchen after you killed Warren, but you couldn't leave someone who might be able to identify you by other means…so, you shot Bennett too."

Natasha O'Connell suddenly began screaming a string of curse words toward Tracy. Thankfully for the detective, he didn't speak Russian. After a moment, she stopped.

"I'm going to provide the police with the information I have, Dr. O'Connell. They will continue the investigation from here. Perhaps there is a motive we don't yet know about. Therefore, I suggest you hire a good lawyer."

Natasha O'Connell started to scream again as her husband addressed Tracy straight on. "I will fight this all the way, Detective Tracy. Shut up, Natasha, get ahold of yourself."

Kenneth O'Connell then turned to the blind man. "...I didn't do this, Uncle Bennett. You must be mistaken." Next, he turned to Warren O'Connell's widow, who looked horrified. "Patsy believe me. I had no reason to kill Uncle Warren. That game was nothing. Everyone knows I was in that accident. And so what if I lied to the police, only Uncle Warren knew what happened. What would I gain by shooting him?

Patsy O'Connell was calm. "I don't know Kenneth. Just take your hysterical wife and go. You have to tell the police the truth. If, as you say, you are innocent, then you have nothing to worry about."

Kenneth O'Connell grabbed for his wife. Natasha was still screaming obscenities at Tracy as they left the kitchen. The front door could be heard slamming behind the retreating couple. And then, all of a sudden, everyone was talking at once. Tracy took his first breath in minutes.

* * *

*"Your life passes before your eyes as you die…
it's called living."*
-T. Pratchett

Before returning home, Detective Tracy sat in the local police headquarters, reviewing some old reports. The motive for the shooting of Bennett and Warren O'Connell was somewhat unclear in his mind. He was curious about what Kenneth O'Connell was so worried about and what incident from 1974 upset him.

And that's when he decided to take it one step further. There were more little game secrets that night before the shooting. He consulted his notes. And then checked each of them, one by one. Some were silly, some frivolous, and three had a sense of mystery. He consulted the local police files after bribing a few officers with a takeout pizza order. Then he looked up all three. Maybe somehow, they were connected. Maybe there was more than one killer. Perhaps the secrets were more important than anyone realized. And that's when he saw it. It was there in black and white, all of the answers. Including the one thing he needed most...a motive for the killing and why Kenneth O'Connell, a well-respected doctor and devoted nephew, would want to see his uncle dead.

* * *

EPILOGUE

"Three blind mice, see how they run."
-T. Ravenscroft, England

Bennett O'Connell came down the stairs. His crutches scraping on the floor. His nurse was taking a shower, and Patsy was off shopping somewhere. He had the house to himself. It had been three days since the police questioned and booked Kenneth O'Connell on murder and attempted murder charges. Yes, things were quiet in the big house. And Bennett O'Connell was healing. Thankfully his wounds were superficial. As Bennett pushed open the door to the kitchen, he sensed he was not alone. *"Oh, those wonderful, heightened senses of a blind man."*

"Sadie, is that you?" he asked. But it wasn't Sadie.

"No, sir. It's Nick. Please come in."

"I didn't know you were still here, Nick. Am I disturbing something?"

"No sir. I'm so glad you came down. I'm conducting a few tests for the investigation. Helping out the local police. I could use your assistance with one of the tests."

Bennett O'Connell lowered himself to a stool as Tracy began. "I have to tell you, sir, I went to the station and went through old police documents. I found some interesting files. I was trying to find a motive for Kenneth O'Connell's actions. And then it hit me...he didn't have one because none existed."

Tracy started to pace around the room. "You were such a big help in this investigation, Bennett. I could never have come up with the killer without your excuse the expression, eye-witness report. Now, I wonder if you would do me a favor and toss this gun for me. Just making a few tests..."

Tracy put a toy gun in the blind man's hand. "Just toss it toward the pantry as you can imagine Kenneth O'Connell did that night."

Bennett O'Connell tossed the toy gun, and it landed with a thud. "Perfect, sir. I was checking the angle. It's just as I thought. Thank you."

Tracy retrieved the toy gun and set it on the counter. "As I mentioned, Bennett, I couldn't have solved this case without your help. The only clues to the killer's identity came from you; without your input, we would have been at a standstill.

"Nick, I don't want to take credit. Kenneth was clearly under a lot of stress. Maybe Warren confronted him about the lie after the game. Maybe he cracked, then waited for my brother to go for his nightly milk and cookies and then took his gun from the study and shot him."

"Ah, yes, sir. Simple. But not that simple."

"What do you mean?"

"It's like this. Kenneth O'Connell didn't kill your brother. It wasn't Kenneth's story during Spill the Beans that set the killer off and made him homicidal. It was another story about a young teenage boy who was caught spying on a girl he was infatuated with—a Peeping Tom. But the girl never gave him a second look. And he must have been furious. She was later found strangled in her front yard. And the killer was never caught. However, one person knew who strangled the young girl. And that night, during Spill the Beans, he hinted as much in front of everyone. Father Flanagan said it was a story about Warren. He had it backward. It was not a story ABOUT Warren but a story told BY Warren."

Tracy took a deep breath. His following words came as if forced out against his will. "...So the killer had to kill him."

"Really, Nick. This sounds like you are fishing."

"No, Bennett. The one thing this investigation lacked was a true motive. And, of course, the fact that we had only your word for everything: The missing tap and the distinctive cologne. The killer knew Warren would be in the kitchen that night—childhood insomnia. Warren was getting too free with their shared secret; he was talking too much. He had to be silenced. The killer shot him and then turned the gun on himself to make it look like he too was an intended victim."

Bennett O'Connell laughed; his head thrown back. "You've lost your mind, Nick. I say you're bluffing."

"If I'm bluffing, sir, it's with the best hand."

"You know this is crazy, and you can't prove a thing."

"No sir, it's not crazy. You took the gun out of the drawer when you came downstairs. And you knew where the four bullets were stored. You shot your brother, shot yourself, and then tossed the gun just as you did a moment ago. I didn't tell you which direction the pantry was just now; I didn't have to because you already knew. And then you invented the story of walking towards the killer to explain the powder residue on your clothes and hands. But as you said yourself, your heightened sense of hearing would have told you right where the killer was standing. I'm sure that while you were in the hospital recovering from your superficial wounds, you had more than enough time to invent all those details about your brother addressing the killer as he entered the kitchen, implying that the killer had something to hide. But the truth is... you were the one with something to hide...

Tracy backed away from the counter. "You heard Kenneth O'Connell walking across the floor that first night. You knew his shoe had a missing tap. And, of course, you detected his cologne. So, you used all those little details to frame him."

"Okay, Nick, maybe you're right, maybe I did it. There was no love lost between my brother and me. He held my accidentally killing that McDonald girl over my head for forty years. He would blackmail me on occasion and get me to do something he wanted. And when I lost my sight a few years ago, he said it served me right. It was my punishment. He kept my secret, alright, but he charged me interest..."

Bennett O'Connell slid off the stool and grabbed for his crutches. "But now that you know, I'm afraid you are out of luck. There's no way for you to prove anything. Never tell the truth when a perfectly good lie will do. So, it's my word against yours, and as I've said on many occasions, everyone feels sorry for a blind man."

Suddenly, a new sound emerged in the kitchen. A rustling. It was the sound of someone moving from the far corner of the room. A blind man will tell you that he can sense another person in the room with him, but he can't identify how many there are.

Officer Jackson of the local police department grabbed Bennett O'Connell's wrist. "You are under arrest Mr. O'Connell. For the murders of Vanessa McDonald and Warren O'Connell. You will be read your rights and then moved to the station for questioning. Please come with me."

Bennett O'Connell reluctantly slipped his crutches under his arms and allowed himself to be lead from the kitchen. Before passing through the door, he turned back, with sightless eyes that knew precisely where his nemesis was standing. "Like I said, Nick, everyone feels sorry for the blind man. It almost worked."

THE HIGH SOCIETY DETECTIVE SERIES

The guest list is exclusive.
The alibis are charming.
The crimes are anything but accidental.

The High Society Detective Series follows a suave, sharp-eyed sleuth through the dark undercurrent of New York's elite— where everyone has something to lose and someone to hide.

ENJOY THE FULL SERIES…
- *The Fourteenth Man at Dinner*
- *Wine, Cheese, and Daggers (Are Back in Style)*
- *The Case of the Wrong Word*

* * *

MORE TITLES COMING SOON
Stay one step ahead of the next crime.

Visit the Amazon Author Page for new releases and updates:
www.amazon.com/author/marilynsporter

ABOUT THE AUTHOR

Marilyn Smith Porter is an American author known for her compelling mystery, suspense, and contemporary fiction. Her novels—including *The High Society Detective Series*, *Last Kiss*, and *Once More*—combine gripping plots with emotional depth and richly drawn characters. Marilyn's stories are filled with intrigue, romance, and unexpected twists that keep readers turning pages late into the night. With a talent for uncovering the extraordinary in everyday moments, she weaves secrets and heart into every story she tells. When she's not writing, Marilyn enjoys traveling, studying history, and discovering the hidden stories woven into real life.

www.ingramcontent.com/pod-product-compliance
Lightning Source LLC
Chambersburg PA
CBHW070633030426
42337CB00020B/4003